# Mogul

**"Rise and Fall"**

by

A. Abney

Published by Double A Publishing 2025

**Contact**

Email: aabney06@aol.com

This book or any portion thereof may not be reproduced or used in any manner whatsoever without the express written permission of the publisher except for the use of brief quotations in a book review.

Copyright ©2025 All rights are reserved.

# Preface

This book is dedicated to the unsung heroes of the streets, the resilient spirits who rise from the ashes of adversity, the dreamers who dare to chase impossible goals despite the odds stacked against them. It's for the mothers who tirelessly work to protect their children from the harsh realities of a world that often seems determined to break them. This is a tribute to the unwavering strength of the human spirit, the capacity for resilience even in the face of unimaginable hardship, and the unwavering belief in the possibility of a better tomorrow.

To those who have known the sting of betrayal, the weight of injustice, and the struggle to maintain their integrity in a world that often seems determined to pull you down – this book is for you. May it serve as a reminder that even in the darkest of times, the human spirit can endure, adapt, and ultimately triumph.

Finally, this is dedicated to the unwavering belief in second chances, in the transformative power of redemption, and in the enduring strength of the human spirit. May this story remind us that even when everything seems lost, there is always the possibility of rebuilding, reimagining, and redefining our place in the world. The path to redemption is not easy, it's often paved with adversity and challenges, but the potential rewards make the journey worthwhile.

# Table of Contents

Chapter 1: From the Streets to the Suites.................................................................. 9

Chapter 2: Unraveling the Truth ...... 53

Chapter 3: Betrayal and Redemption ........................................................................ 95

Chapter 4: Consequences and Reckoning ................................................ 141

Chapter 5: New Beginnings .............. 187

## Chapter 1: From the Streets to the Suites

The air hung thick and heavy with the scent of burnt sugar and desperation. It clung to the threadbare clothes of the children playing hopscotch amidst cracked pavement, the same pavement that served as a canvas for discarded lottery tickets and shattered dreams. This was Big D's Chicago, a city that whispered promises of fortune while simultaneously brandishing the brutal reality of poverty. He was born Demetrius "Big D" Davis into a life where survival was a daily battle fought on streets paved with broken glass and shadowed by the ever-present threat of violence. His mother, a woman of unshakeable strength and quiet dignity, worked tirelessly as a cleaner in a downtown office building, her meager wages barely enough to keep food on the table and a roof over their heads in their cramped, dilapidated apartment.

The building itself, a crumbling testament to neglect, echoed with the sounds of squeaking pipes, leaky faucets, and the muffled cries of neighbors locked in their own struggles. The walls, paper-thin and stained with the grime of decades, offered little privacy. Big D learned early on to tune out the noise, to filter the constant stream of hardship into a background hum against which he could forge his own path. His early childhood memories were not of idyllic playgrounds or family gatherings, but of dodging stray bullets, the chilling shriek of sirens, and the constant anxiety of wondering where the next meal would come from.

His resourcefulness bloomed early. At the age of eight, he was already adept at finding ways to supplement their income, running errands for the neighborhood's more prosperous residents, occasionally engaging in petty theft to fill the gaps. It wasn't a life he chose, but one that chose him, a grim initiation into the realities of the street. He learned the unspoken rules of survival, the complex code of loyalty and betrayal, the delicate dance between avoiding conflict and knowing when to strike. The streets were a harsh teacher, but Big D was a quick study. He learned to read people, to anticipate their moves, to navigate the labyrinthine social dynamics with a shrewdness that belied his age.

His encounters with crime were frequent, not always of his own making. He'd witnessed drug deals gone wrong, brutal muggings, and the chilling aftermath of gang violence. These weren't abstract concepts, distant realities portrayed on television; they were the brutal fabric of his everyday life. He saw the seductive allure of power and the intoxicating promise of quick riches offered by the underworld, but even then, a flicker of something else burned within him – a desperate desire for something more, something beyond the suffocating confines of his immediate reality.

One evening, while scavenging for discarded cans and bottles to recycle for a few extra cents, he stumbled upon a group of teenagers rehearsing hip-hop in an abandoned lot. The raw energy, the rhythmic pulse of the music, and the fierce passion in their eyes resonated deep within him. This was a revelation. This wasn't about survival, this was about creation, about channeling the pain and anger into something beautiful and powerful. It was a form of rebellion, a way to reclaim his narrative from the chaos surrounding him. He started hanging around, absorbing their knowledge, mimicking their movements, finding solace in the shared creative space.

His inherent charisma began to shine through. He possessed a natural magnetism that drew people to him, a combination of street smarts and a raw authenticity that transcended his impoverished surroundings. He became a mediator, resolving minor conflicts, using his skills of persuasion to smooth over tensions between rival factions. It wasn't heroic, but it was a demonstration of leadership, an assertion of his presence. He was more than a survivor; he was a force to be reckoned with, even in his youth.

His mother, despite the constant hardships, remained his unwavering anchor. She didn't condone his dalliances with the darker elements of the neighborhood, but she understood the circumstances that shaped him. Her love was not a suffocating blanket of protection, but a quiet strength that allowed him to navigate the treacherous landscape of his world. She instilled in him a sense of self-worth, a belief in his potential that even he, at times, struggled to believe in himself. She taught him the value of hard work, the importance of perseverance, and the significance of loyalty—qualities that would shape his future success and moral complexity.

The contrast between his mother's unwavering faith and the brutal realities of his environment was stark, creating a duality that would become a defining characteristic of Big D. He developed a ruthless pragmatism, a willingness to do what it took to survive, yet beneath the hardened exterior, a deep-seated empathy for those less fortunate remained. This dichotomy fueled his ambition, pushing him to transcend his circumstances, to create a life that was as different as possible from the one he knew. He saw the music industry not as a source of entertainment but as an escape route, a chance to climb out of the pit he found himself in and drag others with him.

He began to hone his business acumen, trading small favors for larger deals, learning the intricate art of negotiation, and developing an almost preternatural ability to assess risk and seize opportunity. The streets had taught him to anticipate moves, to read people's body language, to sniff out deception. This was an education he couldn't find in any classroom, an education that proved more valuable than any degree from a prestigious university. He learned to leverage his street cred, building relationships with other hustlers and developing a network of contacts that extended far beyond his immediate neighborhood.

As he got older, his involvement in less savory activities intensified, though always with a clear goal in mind: accumulating enough capital to launch his own venture, a path towards financial independence. He understood the necessity of playing the game by its own brutal rules, adapting his strategy to every turn, but always with his eyes fixed on the prize – a future that promised something far beyond the grimy streets of his youth. He was never afraid to push boundaries, to walk the tightrope between legality and criminality. But always, beneath the layers of ambition and ruthlessness, there was a yearning for something legitimate, a desire to build something lasting, something that could stand as a monument to his resilience and tenacity.

The pivotal moments of his early life weren't single, dramatic events but rather a slow accumulation of experiences that gradually shaped his personality and defined his trajectory. Each small victory, each narrow escape, each betrayal and act of loyalty, contributed to the creation of Demetrius "Big D" Davis – the ambitious, ruthless, charismatic, and ultimately, complex man who would rise from the poverty-stricken streets of Chicago to become a powerful force in the music industry. The streets had given him an education that no university could match; the hardships had forged his spirit, making him both resilient and formidable. His journey was far from over, but the foundations had been laid, a testament to the enduring power of ambition and the unshakeable strength of a mother's love in a world where survival was the ultimate test of character. He was ready. The streets had prepared him. Now, it was time to conquer the world.

The seed of Big D Records wasn't planted in a boardroom, but on the cracked asphalt of a South Side Chicago parking lot. It started not with a grand business plan, but with a beat – a raw, visceral rhythm pulsing from a boombox, spitting out lyrics that spoke of struggle, ambition, and the raw energy of the streets. Big D, still navigating the treacherous currents of the underground, saw something more than just music; he saw potential, raw talent waiting to be harnessed. He saw opportunity.

His first artist, a fiery young rapper named J-Roc, was a walking embodiment of the streets, his rhymes dripping with the harsh realities of poverty and violence. J-Roc was rough around the edges, his talent undeniable but overshadowed by his volatile personality and a penchant for trouble. Big D saw past the flaws, recognizing the magnetic force of J-Roc's music. He saw the hunger in his eyes, the burning desire to escape, a hunger that mirrored his own.

Their initial collaboration was a testament to Big D's intuitive understanding of the music business. He didn't just manage J-Roc; he mentored him, honing his raw talent, channeling his aggressive energy into focused creativity. He secured a low-budget recording session in a cramped, dimly lit studio, a far cry from the polished environments of major labels. The resulting tracks were raw, authentic, imbued with a street credibility that major labels couldn't manufacture.

The distribution strategy was as unconventional as the music itself. Big D leveraged his network of contacts, his deep understanding of the city's underground currents. He bypassed the established channels, working directly with street vendors, independent record stores, and underground clubs. He understood the importance of word-of-mouth, the power of street cred in building a genuine following. J-Roc's music became the soundtrack of the streets, spreading organically, generating a buzz that could no longer be ignored.

The initial success with J-Roc provided the foundation for Big D's burgeoning empire. He reinvested every penny back into the business, meticulously managing expenses, always looking for the next opportunity. He didn't just sign artists; he built relationships, becoming a mentor, a confidante, a shrewd business partner. He learned the intricacies of the music industry by doing, by making mistakes, by learning from them. He studied contracts, negotiated deals, and built alliances with key players in the local scene.

Building Big D Records wasn't just about music; it was about networking. He cultivated relationships with club owners, DJs, promoters, and other influential figures in the Chicago music scene.

He understood the importance of fostering a sense of community, of building a network that supported and promoted each other's success. It wasn't a hierarchical structure; it was a collaborative ecosystem. He fostered a sense of loyalty and mutual respect, which proved invaluable in the cutthroat world of the music industry.

The expansion of Big D Records wasn't linear; it was a series of calculated risks, strategic partnerships, and hard-fought victories. He faced numerous setbacks, near misses, and betrayals. He learned to trust his gut, to recognize when an opportunity was too good to be true. He negotiated deals that were both lucrative and fair, always aiming for a win-win scenario that fostered long-term relationships. He learned the importance of legal advice, engaging attorneys early on to ensure that his business was operating within legal parameters. He understood that the lines between legality and criminality were often blurred in his world, but he always strived to operate on the right side of the law.

One crucial partnership was with a seasoned lawyer, Ms. Ava Ramirez, who became more than just his legal counsel; she became a trusted advisor, guiding him through the complex legal landscape of the music industry, helping him navigate the treacherous waters of copyright, contracts, and intellectual property rights. Ms. Ramirez's insights proved invaluable, helping Big D avoid costly mistakes and build a sustainable business model. Her pragmatic approach complimented his street smarts, creating a powerful synergy that steered Big D Records through many a potential legal minefield.

Big D's leadership style was a fascinating paradox. He was both ruthless and empathetic, demanding but supportive. He instilled a sense of loyalty in his employees, creating a culture of hard work and dedication. He recognized talent, nurtured it, and provided the resources and support necessary for his artists to flourish. He also demanded excellence, holding his team accountable for their performance. There was no room for slackers in his organization.

He embraced the ever-evolving nature of the music industry. He was among the first to understand the impact of the internet and digital distribution. He invested in new technologies, adapting to the changing landscape and securing the label's place in the new digital world. This forward-thinking approach, coupled with his shrewd business acumen, cemented Big D Records' position as a major player in the industry.

The success wasn't without conflict. Rival labels tried to undercut him, competitors attempted to steal his artists, and there were moments when the sheer weight of his ambition almost crushed him. But Big D persevered, fueled by his unwavering determination and the loyalty of his team. He learned to adapt, to overcome obstacles, and to use his setbacks as fuel for his relentless pursuit of success.

The early years of Big D Records were a whirlwind of late nights, tense negotiations, and constant hustling. He built his empire from the ground up, brick by brick, sweat and grit forming the foundation. His unwavering focus was on building a legacy, not just a business. He wanted to create a platform that allowed artists to realize their full potential, to tell their stories, and to share their unique voices with the world. He wanted to provide a path for others to escape the same streets that had shaped him. His vision extended beyond the bottom line; he saw Big D Records as a force for positive change, a vehicle for empowerment.

Big D's rise wasn't simply about money and success. It was about proving that even amidst the poverty and violence, dreams could be realized, that talent could emerge from the most unlikely of places. He was building more than a record label; he was building a testament to resilience, a monument to the power of perseverance. His journey was a story of grit, determination, and the unwavering belief in the transformative power of music. And as his label grew, so too did his influence, his name synonymous with both success and a certain enigmatic, untouchable aura, a testament to the man who'd built his empire from the streets of Chicago. But little did he know this very success would soon become the target of scrutiny, threatening to unravel everything he'd worked so hard to achieve.

Serena's voice, a smoky contralto that could melt asphalt and shatter glass, was the soundtrack to Big D Records' ascension. Before her, the label had been a scrappy underdog, clawing its way to recognition. With Serena, it became a force to be reckoned with, a powerhouse that commanded attention. Her discovery wasn't a matter of chance, but of keen observation. Big D, during a late-night scouting mission at a dimly lit, smoke-filled club on the city's West Side, had heard her – a raw, untamed talent hidden amidst a crowd of boisterous patrons. He'd seen the way she commanded the stage, the passion that burned in her eyes, a fire that mirrored his own ambition.

She was the antithesis of J-Roc; polished yet fiercely independent, a woman who knew exactly what she wanted and wasn't afraid to grab it. Where J-Roc was a product of the streets, radiating raw energy, Serena was a carefully sculpted masterpiece, a singer who possessed both natural talent and an almost unnerving self-awareness. She had a backstory, a narrative as compelling as her voice: a childhood marred by poverty and neglect, a relentless drive to escape the confines of her circumstances. This resonated deeply with Big D; he saw a reflection of his own struggles in her determined eyes.

Their initial collaboration was a whirlwind. Big D, having refined his methods over the years, secured a state-of-the-art recording studio, a far cry from the cramped, dimly lit spaces of his earlier ventures. He surrounded Serena with the best; seasoned producers, meticulous engineers, and a team dedicated to crafting her image. He didn't just manage her; he mentored her, guiding her through the complexities of the music industry, shielding her from the pitfalls that could easily derail a young artist's career. He invested heavily in her, ensuring she had the best clothes, the best stylists, and the best support system. He understood the power of image, the crucial role it played in building a successful career. He molded her, not into something artificial, but into the best version of herself – a diamond he'd unearthed from the rough.

The first single was an instant hit. It climbed the charts with breathtaking speed, its infectious rhythm and Serena's powerful vocals resonating with a generation yearning for authenticity. The accompanying music video, shot in a stylized blend of urban grit and glamorous elegance, showcased both her talent and her striking beauty. Big D understood the power of visual media, the importance of creating a compelling visual narrative that complemented the music. He ensured the video captured the essence of Serena's story, her journey from the streets to the bright lights of the stage.

The success of the first single catapulted Serena into the spotlight. Her concerts became legendary, sold-out affairs filled with a sea of adoring fans. The media showered her with attention, painting her as the next big thing, the voice of a generation. She became a symbol of hope, inspiration, proof that dreams could come true, even in the face of overwhelming adversity. Her story mirrored Big D's own, a testament to the transformative power of music and sheer determination.

Big D reveled in her success. He saw it as a validation of his instincts, a testament to his ability to identify and nurture raw talent. He basked in the glow of her fame, proudly showcasing her as the jewel in the crown of his burgeoning empire. He enjoyed the lavish parties, the exclusive events, the champagne toasts, all testaments to his and Serena's hard work and mutual success. But beneath the surface, a subtle tension began to emerge.

As Serena's fame grew, so did her independence. She started asserting her creative control, pushing the boundaries of her image, challenging Big D's decisions. Her ambition, once a shared flame, now seemed to burn hotter than his own. The power dynamic, once clearly defined, started to shift, creating an undercurrent of unease between them. She began surrounding herself with her own team, advisors, and managers, creating a space between herself and Big D, a subtle detachment that he couldn't quite comprehend.

Big D, used to being the sole architect of his own success, found himself adapting to Serena's growing autonomy. He tried to maintain control, but he also recognized the value of her independence. He understood that to stifle her creativity would be to stifle her success, and her success was intrinsically linked to his own. He walked a precarious line, balancing his desire for control with the necessity of supporting her artistic vision. He provided the resources, the platform, the infrastructure, but increasingly she was making the creative choices.

Their conflicting personalities began to clash. Big D, the street-smart hustler, remained grounded in the reality of their shared beginnings. He valued loyalty, hard work, and a sense of mutual respect. Serena, polished and sophisticated, existed in a different realm, a world of glamour, ambition, and relentless pursuit of self-expression. Her desires were not only artistic but also financial, a driving force that sometimes led to friction with Big D's business sensibilities. She wanted more control over her image, more say in her financial deals, a greater share of the profits. She wanted to transcend the role of simply a singer for the label. She wanted ownership of her own destiny.

The contrast in their backgrounds created a subtle divide. Big D's roots remained firmly planted in the streets, while Serena, despite her humble origins, had embraced the glamorous lifestyle of a pop star. This difference in perspective fueled their subtle conflicts, shaping their professional interactions, often resulting in strained conversations and tense negotiations. He saw the world through the lens of risk and reward, calculating each move, weighing the pros and cons. She, on the other hand, operated with a bolder, more intuitive approach, her gut feeling often guiding her decisions.

Their collaboration became a delicate dance, a carefully orchestrated balance between their diverging personalities and ambitious goals. The friction between them, though largely unspoken, was palpable. The lavish parties, once celebratory occasions, now felt charged with a different energy, the underlying tension casting a shadow over the glittering facade. While outwardly their partnership appeared flawless, a chasm was slowly forming, a silent fracture that threatened to shatter the carefully constructed image of their success. The seeds of discord had been sown, and the harvest would soon be reaped. The glamorous world of music, with its dazzling lights and intoxicating allure, was masking a brewing storm, a conflict that threatened to destroy not only their partnership but also Big D's carefully constructed empire. The question lingered: could their shared success withstand the strain of their diverging ambitions and conflicting personalities?

The whispers started subtly, like the hiss of a leaky pipe in a mansion otherwise brimming with opulence. At first, Big D dismissed them. He'd built his empire on grit and determination, weathering storms far fiercer than a few disgruntled whispers. But these whispers weren't coming from the streets; they were emanating from within his own gilded cage, from the very people he trusted.

It began with small things. A misplaced invoice, a suspiciously altered contract, a late-night phone call intercepted by a sharp-eared assistant. Each incident, individually insignificant, added up to a growing sense of unease. He'd always operated on instinct, his gut a reliable compass guiding him through the treacherous waters of the music industry. Now, his gut was churning, a storm brewing beneath the calm exterior of his meticulously crafted success.

The tension with Serena wasn't just creative differences anymore. It had morphed into something colder, more calculated. Her requests for more control – over her image, her finances, her creative direction – were no longer polite negotiations but demands. She'd assembled her own team of lawyers and managers, a shadow cabinet mirroring Big D's own organization, yet operating independently, even secretively at times. The once-open lines of communication had narrowed to tight, guarded exchanges.

He noticed the change in her demeanor, the subtle shift in her gaze. The fiery passion that had once burned so brightly in her eyes now flickered, replaced by a cool, calculating intelligence. Her smile, once spontaneous and genuine, now felt forced, a carefully constructed mask concealing something he couldn't quite decipher. She still performed flawlessly on stage, her voice a weapon of mass seduction, but backstage, she was a different woman altogether – reserved, guarded, almost hostile.

The cracks weren't just appearing between him and Serena; they were spreading across his entire organization. Loyalty, once the bedrock of Big D Records, seemed to be eroding. He caught snippets of conversations, overheard hushed arguments, witnessed furtive glances exchanged across boardroom tables. Old alliances shifted, loyalties wavered. He started suspecting that some of his closest associates were feeding information to the media, subtly manipulating the narrative to their advantage.

J-Roc, his longtime friend and street-savvy manager, seemed oddly distant, his usual boisterous energy dampened by a newfound reticence. He'd always been Big D's eyes and ears on the streets, a vital link to the pulse of the city, but now, even J-Roc's loyalty felt questionable. There were whispers of J-Roc secretly negotiating side deals, of him skimming profits from the label. While J-Roc was still superficially supportive, his demeanor shifted, and the bond they'd forged on the streets felt brittle, ready to shatter.

The media, ever hungry for scandal, began to hone in on the cracks, amplifying the whispers into full-blown accusations. Rival record labels, sensing weakness, launched aggressive smear campaigns. Articles questioning Big D's business practices, his past dealings, and the ethical implications of his success began to surface in major publications. The once-unassailable image of Big D, the self-made mogul, started to crumble under the weight of these attacks.

He fought back, employing his formidable legal team to quell the damaging articles, but the attacks persisted, unrelenting and relentless. The whispers had become a roar, a deafening chorus of accusations, fueled by rumors and innuendo. He was portrayed not as a visionary entrepreneur but as a ruthless opportunist, a man who'd risen to success on the backs of others. His hard-earned reputation, the foundation of his empire, was being systematically dismantled.

The pressure mounted. Sleep became a luxury he couldn't afford. He found himself consumed by a constant state of paranoia, second-guessing everyone, questioning every loyalty. The lavish parties, the champagne toasts, had lost their luster. The opulent suites felt cold and isolating, the once vibrant atmosphere replaced by a sense of suffocating dread. He'd traded the harsh realities of the streets for a new kind of hardship – the relentless pressure of defending his empire against enemies both internal and external.

Then, the feds arrived. It wasn't a dramatic raid, no flashing lights or shouting agents. Instead, it was a quiet, formal summons. A polite request to appear for questioning regarding allegations of financial irregularities and potential tax evasion. It wasn't the first time he'd dealt with the authorities; in his past, he'd navigated countless encounters with the law, using his street smarts to evade prosecution. But this was different. This was a full-scale investigation, an indication of the extent to which the whispers had grown into accusations. This was a challenge to his very existence, a threat to everything he'd painstakingly built.

The arrival of the feds marked a significant turning point. The whispers of betrayal had become a deafening roar; the subtle cracks in his empire had widened into gaping fissures. The luxurious facade of his success had crumbled, revealing a core of uncertainty, fear, and mistrust. The fight for his empire, his freedom, and his reputation was no longer a subtle struggle; it was an all-out war. His once impeccable image was now a battlefield, scarred by accusations and riddled with doubt. The stakes were higher than ever; his hard-earned empire, built on sweat, ambition, and a relentless drive to succeed, hung precariously in the balance. The game had changed, and Big D knew he was playing for keeps. He'd faced down street thugs and ruthless competitors, but this battle – against the relentless power of the federal government and the insidious betrayals within his own organization – would be his greatest challenge yet. The journey from the streets to the suites had brought him untold wealth and power, but it had also exposed him to a new, more dangerous kind of threat, a threat that could obliterate everything he'd worked so hard to achieve. He was no longer fighting for success; he was fighting for survival.

The summons arrived on a Tuesday, delivered not with the theatrical flourish of a police raid, but with the quiet efficiency of a well-oiled machine. A crisp, official-looking envelope, bearing the seal of the Department of Justice, landed on Big D's mahogany desk, interrupting a meeting about Serena's upcoming album launch. The room, usually alive with the energy of creative ambition, fell silent. The air, thick with the scent of expensive coffee and simmering tension, grew colder.

Big D, his face a mask of controlled composure, opened the envelope. His eyes, usually sharp and calculating, narrowed as he scanned the formal request for an interview regarding "allegations of financial impropriety and potential tax evasion." The polite language belied the gravity of the situation. This wasn't a minor infraction; this was a full-blown federal investigation, a threat that could unravel his meticulously built empire in a matter of weeks.

The initial shock gave way to a surge of adrenaline. Big D, a man who'd clawed his way out of the brutal streets of Chicago, wasn't easily intimidated. He'd faced down gangbangers, outwitted rivals, and navigated the treacherous currents of the music industry for years. But this was different. This wasn't a street fight; this was a legal war, one he couldn't win with fists or street smarts alone.

He called Marcus, his lead lawyer, a man whose calm demeanor was as reassuring as a sturdy fortress. Marcus, a seasoned veteran of high-stakes legal battles, arrived within the hour, his briefcase a silent symbol of legal power. His face, usually jovial, was etched with concern. The air in Marcus's sterile, high-rise office was different from Big D's opulent suite. Here, the scent of expensive leather and polished mahogany was replaced by the sharp, antiseptic smell of legal formality; a place where power resided not in creative genius, but in meticulous documentation and strategic maneuvering.

The next few hours were a blur of frantic activity. Phones rang incessantly, a cacophony of legal jargon and panicked voices. Big D, despite the pressure, remained outwardly calm, a master puppeteer orchestrating his defense. He instructed his team to gather every financial record, every contract, every invoice – a mountain of paperwork documenting years of hard work and relentless ambition. He needed to prove his innocence; to show the feds that his empire was built on legitimate success, not shady dealings.

The news spread like wildfire through Big D Records. The whispers, once confined to hushed corners and anxious glances, exploded into a full-blown panic. Fear, raw and palpable, hung in the air like a suffocating blanket. The staff, once buzzing with the energy of a thriving record label, moved with a subdued anxiety, their faces etched with uncertainty. The creative energy that once pulsed through the office was replaced by a chilling silence, broken only by the clicking of keyboards and the muffled sounds of anxious phone calls.

The artists, Big D's prized possessions, were equally unsettled. Serena, the source of the initial whispers, remained elusive, her lawyer acting as a shield between her and the swirling chaos. The other artists, sensing the instability, became increasingly agitated, their contracts and career trajectories hanging precariously in the balance. The atmosphere of creative collaboration and mutual support that had once defined Big D Records was shattered, replaced by a tense atmosphere of self-preservation.

Big D, meanwhile, shifted between the sterile environment of Marcus's office and the opulent, yet now unsettling, comfort of his own suite. His normally pristine office, a symbol of his success, felt like a cage, the walls closing in on him. The opulent furniture, the breathtaking city view – all seemed to mock his current predicament. The once-vibrant, high-energy atmosphere was gone, replaced by a heavy silence, punctuated only by the incessant buzz of his phone and the rhythmic tapping of his fingers on the mahogany desk.

He needed to understand the source of the accusation. Was Serena the mastermind, using her position to leverage a better deal? Or was this a carefully orchestrated attack from a rival label, aiming to bring down his empire? He'd built this from nothing, survived the streets, and the cutthroat business world of music, but this challenge felt different. This was a battle not just against his rivals, but against the seemingly unstoppable power of the federal government. His street smarts would only take him so far; he needed a different kind of strategy, a sophisticated defense worthy of the formidable opponent he faced.

He ventured into the seedier parts of Chicago, places where the lights were dimmer, the faces harder, and loyalties were bought and sold. He met with old contacts, people who knew the underbelly of the city, the places where secrets were buried and deals were made. He needed intelligence, information that could help him understand the scope of the investigation, the players involved, and ultimately, the truth behind the accusations.

The city, once a source of inspiration and opportunity, now felt like a labyrinth of shadows and uncertainty. The city that had once embraced him as a hero, a self-made mogul who rose from the streets to conquer the industry, was now watching him with a mixture of curiosity and skepticism. The weight of expectation, the pressure of his empire, and the threat of imprisonment pressed down on him, turning the once-familiar streets into a hostile landscape.

The fight for his empire was no longer a battle for success; it was a desperate fight for survival. The journey from the streets to the suites had brought him unimaginable wealth and power, but it had also exposed him to a new level of danger, a world where the rules were different, the stakes were higher, and betrayal lurked around every corner. The game had changed, and Big D knew that this time, he was playing for keeps. His future, his freedom, his entire empire, rested on the delicate balance of truth, loyalty, and the ever-present shadow of the federal investigation. The whispers were gone, replaced by the heavy silence of looming danger. The war had begun.

## Chapter 2: Unraveling the Truth

The lead investigator, Agent Parker, a woman whose steely gaze could cut through the most hardened criminal, poured over the financial records. Mountains of paperwork sprawled across her desk, a testament to Big D's sprawling empire. Each document, meticulously examined, whispered a story – a story of lavish spending, questionable investments, and a network of shell corporations that seemed designed to obfuscate rather than illuminate. Parker wasn't easily impressed; she'd seen it all before, the carefully constructed facades masking illicit dealings. But Big D's case was different. The sheer scale of his operation, the audacity of his alleged schemes, was breathtaking.

She focused on a series of complex transactions involving offshore accounts, meticulously disguised to avoid detection. The paper trail led to a network of shell companies registered in tax havens; each linked to Big D's various business ventures. It was a labyrinthine structure, designed to conceal the true source of funds and the ultimate beneficiaries. Parker felt the thrill of the chase, the intellectual challenge of untangling the web of deceit. This wasn't just about numbers; it was about power, influence, and the corrosive effects of unchecked ambition.

Meanwhile, Big D, in the dimly lit confines of a backroom bar, sat across from Frankie "The Fixer" Moretti, a man whose reputation preceded him. Frankie, with his shrewd eyes and a network of informants that extended into every corner of the city, was Big D's last resort. He'd seen Big D rise from the streets, a journey he'd both admired and envied. Now, he was offering his services, a lifeline in a sea of legal turmoil.

"Serena," Frankie said, his voice a low growl, "she's playing a dangerous game. Someone's pulling her strings." Big D leaned forward, his gaze intense. "Who?"

Frankie shrugged. "That's what I'm trying to find out. But it ain't just Serena. There's more to this than meets the eye. People are afraid, Big D. Afraid of what you know, afraid of what you might reveal."

The conversation continued late into the night, a clandestine exchange of information in a world where trust was a rare commodity. Frankie revealed whispers of a long-standing rivalry with a rival record label, a bitter feud fueled by jealousy and ambition. This rival, a ruthless mogul named Victor "The Viper"

Rossi, had the resources and the motive to orchestrate Serena's accusations.

The following days were a whirlwind of activity. Parker's team, working tirelessly, uncovered evidence of questionable accounting practices, inflated invoices, and payments to individuals whose identities were deliberately obscured. They discovered a pattern of suspicious transactions; all connected to the same offshore accounts identified earlier. It was a carefully crafted scheme, designed to siphon off millions in untaxed profits. Parker suspected money laundering, and this wasn't just small-time; it was sophisticated, involving international banking institutions and shell companies spread across multiple jurisdictions.

Big D, meanwhile, was building his defense. He met with his legal team, going over each piece of evidence, anticipating the prosecution's case. Marcus, his lawyer, was concerned, but he remained optimistic. He believed that Big D's success story was a testament to his hard work, and he was determined to prove his client's innocence.

The investigation expanded, reaching beyond the immediate circle of Big D Records. Parker's team interviewed former employees, artists, and business associates, unearthing a trail of past indiscretions, shady deals, and hidden alliances. The picture that emerged was far more complex than initially anticipated, a tapestry of ambition, betrayal, and revenge. The deeper they dug, the more secrets they unearthed, secrets that threatened to topple not just Big D's empire, but potentially the entire industry.

One crucial piece of evidence came from an unexpected source: a disgruntled former employee, once loyal to Big D, now bitter and resentful after a falling out. He revealed a hidden ledger detailing unreported income, illicit payments to corrupt officials, and a secret offshore account controlled by Big D. This information, kept hidden for years, provided the missing link, solidifying the case against Big D.

The pressure mounted. Big D, once the king of his domain, found himself increasingly isolated, his once-loyal team wavering. The once-vibrant atmosphere of his record label had been replaced by suspicion and fear. The artists, once eager to please, were now distancing themselves, their careers hanging precariously in the balance.

Serena, the trigger of this whole crisis, remained elusive. Her lawyer, a master of obfuscation, skillfully avoided any direct confrontation, allowing the storm to rage around her. Yet, subtle hints hinted at a deeper conflict, a personal grievance that extended beyond a simple contract dispute. The investigators learned of a long-standing tension between Serena and Big D, a clash of egos and ambition, a power struggle that had been simmering beneath the surface for years.

The investigation deepened, revealing a web of connections that extended far beyond Big D Records. It exposed a culture of corruption within the music industry, a world where deals were made in smoky backrooms, where loyalty was bought and sold, and where the line between right and wrong had long since been blurred. Parker felt a growing sense of disillusionment, a realization that the seemingly glamorous world of music was riddled with darkness, its allure masking a grim reality of power struggles, betrayals, and illicit dealings.

Big D, facing overwhelming evidence, knew his empire was crumbling. He was trapped in a web of his own making, a victim of his unchecked ambition and the ruthless nature of the industry he had conquered. The fight for his survival was not merely a legal battle; it was a fight against the shadows of his own past, the secrets he had buried deep beneath the glittering facade of success. His rise from the streets had been brutal, and now, he faced the possibility of a fall even more devastating. The game, once played with such confidence and skill, had turned against him, and the stakes were higher than ever. The truth, long hidden, was finally emerging, revealing a reality far more complex and dangerous than anyone had anticipated. The investigation had just begun to scratch the surface, and the final chapter of Big D's story remained unwritten, hanging precariously in the balance.

The chipped paint on the studio wall seemed to mock Serena's carefully constructed image. She traced the cracks with a manicured fingernail, the stark contrast a mirror of her own fractured reality. The glitz and glamour of her recent success felt like a distant memory; a cruel joke played on her by a system that had devoured her innocence and left her scarred.

It hadn't started this way. The initial thrill of signing with Big D Records had been intoxicating. She'd been a nobody, a girl with a voice that could melt asphalt, singing in smoky bars for spare change. Big D had seen something in her, something raw and untamed, and he'd offered her a chance, a pathway to a life she'd only dared to dream of.

He'd painted a picture of empowerment, of artistic freedom, of building a legacy. He'd promised her the world, and for a while, she'd believed him. The lavish recording sessions, the designer clothes, the whirlwind of promotional events – it had all been exhilarating, a dizzying ascent into a world of luxury she'd never known.

But the cracks appeared early. Subtle at first, then widening into chasms that threatened to swallow her whole. The initial enthusiasm of her team slowly transformed into a calculated control. Her creative input was dismissed, her opinions ignored. Big D, the once-charismatic mentor, became increasingly demanding, his praise turning to criticism, his suggestions morphing into orders.

The subtle shifts in the contract terms went unnoticed at first, buried within pages of legal jargon. But the implications were devastating. Her share of the profits dwindled, her creative freedom eroded. She was a commodity, a cash cow to be milked dry. Her voice, her art, her very essence, were being manipulated and exploited for the benefit of Big D's empire.

Then came the insistent advances, veiled as professional advice, as opportunities for networking. The constant pressure, the thinly veiled threats, the suffocating atmosphere of intimidation. She learned to navigate the tightrope walk of maintaining professional composure while battling the creeping sense of fear that gnawed at her confidence.

She wasn't alone. She began to see similar patterns in the experiences of other female artists on the label. Whispers in the hallways, hushed conversations in dimly lit corners, shared experiences of exploitation and manipulation. They were all pawns in Big D's game, their talents exploited, their voices silenced.

One night, after a particularly grueling promotional event, a seasoned singer, a woman who had weathered years in the industry, pulled Serena aside. Her eyes, etched with years of unspoken pain, conveyed a silent understanding.

"Honey," she said, her voice a low rasp, "you think you're climbing the ladder, but you're already trapped in the cage. He'll keep you glittering, but he'll never let you truly fly."

The older singer's words struck Serena like a cold wave, shattering the facade of her gilded cage. She realized she wasn't just a victim; she was part of a systematic pattern, a cog in a machine designed to extract maximum profit at the expense of its artists.

Her anger became a burning fire, fueled by years of suppressed resentment and frustration. She started to gather evidence, meticulously documenting every instance of exploitation, every instance of disrespect. Emails, contracts, financial statements, whispered conversations, all served as pieces of a puzzle that revealed the dark underbelly of Big D's glittering empire.

The sexism was rampant, subtle and insidious. Her ideas were often dismissed or credited to male colleagues. Her input during creative meetings was ignored, her concerns brushed aside with patronizing smiles and dismissive remarks. Her worth was constantly undervalued, her compensation dramatically lower than her male counterparts, despite her exceeding all expectations. The pressure to conform to unrealistic beauty standards was relentless, her image meticulously crafted and controlled by Big D's team, transforming her into a manufactured image rather than her authentic self.

As she pieced together the evidence, she realized that her own story was only one thread in a larger tapestry of exploitation. The label was riddled with systemic issues, from unequal pay to unfair contracts, from sexual harassment to blatant disregard for artists' mental well-being. Her fight became more than a personal battle; it became a crusade for the rights and recognition of every woman in the industry.

She knew it wouldn't be easy. Big D was a powerful man, a man whose influence extended beyond the music industry. He had built an empire on the backs of vulnerable artists, and he wouldn't surrender his power without a fight. But Serena, armed with her truth and a newfound resolve, was ready to face him, to expose his hypocrisy and to fight for her freedom, her voice, and the future of countless other women who had suffered in silence. Her accusations weren't just about money or fame; they were about justice, about reclaiming her dignity and her art. It was a fight for her soul, and she was ready to fight to the very end. The fear was still there, a constant companion, but it was overshadowed by a righteous anger that fueled her every action. This fight was bigger than her; it was for every woman who had ever been silenced, exploited, and underestimated in a male-dominated industry. This was a battle for change, a fight for the future of music itself. And Serena, though bruised and battered, was ready to fight.

The road ahead would be treacherous, filled with legal battles, public scrutiny, and the constant threat of retaliation. But Serena was prepared. She had gathered the evidence, she had found her allies, and she had found her voice. She was no longer a frightened girl singing in smoky bars; she was a warrior, ready to take on the Goliath of the music industry. The fight had just begun, and Serena was ready to fight for her truth, for her rights, and for the future of all the women who would follow in her footsteps. Her story was a testament to the resilience of the human spirit, a beacon of hope in the dark corners of the music industry. It was a tale of exploitation, yes, but it was also a testament to the indomitable power of one woman's courage, a courageous battle cry for justice, for equality, and for the right to live authentically and free.

The mahogany desk in Big D's opulent office felt cold beneath his fingertips. The city lights, usually a source of inspiration and pride, now seemed to mock him, their glittering brilliance a stark contrast to the darkness closing in. Serena's accusations weren't just a threat to his empire; they were a crack in the meticulously constructed façade of his carefully curated life. His loyalty, once a fortress, was now crumbling, brick by brick.

Marcus, his right-hand man since the early days, sat opposite him, his usual jovial demeanor replaced by a strained silence. Marcus had seen

Big D at his lowest, had witnessed his rise from the streets, had shared in the triumphs and the heartbreaks. Their bond, forged in the crucible of shared hardship, was the bedrock of Big D's operation, a loyalty built on years of mutual trust and respect. But even Marcus's unwavering loyalty was showing cracks under the immense pressure of the federal investigation.

"This Serena…she's gone rogue," Marcus said finally, his voice low and gravelly, the words hanging heavy in the air. "She's throwing everything we've built under the bus."

Big D leaned back in his chair, the leather creaking beneath his weight. "She's not just throwing us under the bus, Marcus. She's trying to run us over." He ran a hand through his thinning hair, the weariness etched deep in his face. "I gave her everything. A shot, a platform, the chance to make something of herself. And this is how she repays me?"

"Loyalty's a rare commodity these days, D," Marcus countered, his gaze steady. "Especially in this game. Some folks, they'll sell their grandma for a bigger cut."

Big D knew this was true. He'd built his empire on ruthless ambition, on exploiting the weaknesses of others. He'd played the game, and he'd won, but now the game was turning against him, the stakes higher than ever before. He'd underestimated Serena, misjudged her strength, and now he was paying the price.

The betrayal wasn't just coming from Serena. Whispers had begun to circulate within his inner circle. CJ, his head of A&R, a man known for his sharp eye for talent and his even sharper tongue, was suddenly tight-lipped, his usual bravado replaced by a cautious silence. There were subtle shifts in his demeanor, a newfound hesitancy in his eyes, a carefully guarded distance in his interactions. CJ had always been ambitious, but his ambition had always been directed towards Big D's success. Now, it seemed his ambition was pointed toward his own survival.

Then there was Veronica, his long-time lawyer and confidante. A woman known for her ironclad resolve and her unflinching loyalty, she was growing increasingly distant, her legal advice laced with a newfound caution, her reassurances sounding hollow and unconvincing. She was maneuvering carefully, hedging her bets, ensuring her own safety.

Big D realized the weight of his actions. The relentless pressure to succeed, the constant pursuit of wealth and power, had driven a wedge between him and the people he once considered family. He'd created a culture of fear and intimidation, where loyalty was bought and sold, and betrayal was the ultimate currency. Now, he was reaping the consequences of his own ruthlessness.

The federal investigation wasn't just about Serena's accusations; it was a deep dive into the underbelly of Big D's operation, a meticulous examination of his business practices, his contracts, his relationships. The investigators were relentless, their questions probing, their scrutiny intense. Each passing day revealed more cracks in the carefully crafted image he'd cultivated over years.

He was surrounded by people who had climbed aboard the Big D train during its ascent, enjoying the perks and prestige his empire offered. Now, as the train derailed, they were scrambling to find the emergency exits, leaping ship before the wreckage engulfed them all. He realized the harsh truth: in the cutthroat world of the music industry, true loyalty was as rare as a genuine diamond in a pawn shop.

He summoned his entire executive team to a tense meeting. The atmosphere crackled with unspoken anxieties. The faces around the table were a mixture of fear, calculation, and begrudging loyalty. Each member of the team was navigating their own personal crisis, weighing the risks of loyalty against the rewards of self-preservation. The silence was thick enough to cut with a knife.

Big D addressed them directly. "Look, I know this is rough. Serena's accusations…the investigation…it's a mess. But we're going to weather this. We're a team. We stick together, we fight this together. Right?" His voice wavered slightly, a crack in the typically unwavering facade. He needed their support, not just for his business, but for his sanity.

The silence lingered. Each person present was carefully calculating their response, weighing their own survival against years of association with a man who had made them powerful. CJ shifted uncomfortably in his seat, avoiding eye contact. Veronica offered a stiff nod, her expression inscrutable. Only Marcus maintained his steady gaze, his loyalty unwavering despite the overwhelming pressure.

The meeting ended without a concrete plan, a testament to the crumbling trust and shifting loyalties that now defined Big D's inner circle. The ensuing days were a blur of legal maneuvers, damage control, and frantic attempts to salvage his reputation. But the damage was done. The once-impregnable fortress of his empire was now riddled with cracks, the foundations weakened by the betrayals of those he once considered his allies.

Big D was alone, isolated at the top of his collapsing empire, surrounded by a cast of self-serving individuals, each one focused on their own survival in the wake of his downfall. The truth, like a relentless tide, was beginning to expose the dark undercurrents that flowed beneath the surface of Big D's success. His ascent had been built on a foundation of ambition and ruthlessness, and now, that same ambition and ruthlessness were tearing everything he had built to shreds. The fight for his survival was not only against the feds, but against the very people who had helped him build his empire, now desperately fighting for their own lives amidst the wreckage. The loyalties he had cultivated, once rock solid, had crumbled under the pressure, revealing the bitter truth: in the cutthroat world of music and power, there were no true allies, only enemies waiting for their moment to strike.

The weight of the federal investigation pressed down on Big D like a physical force. Sleep became a luxury he couldn't afford, his nights filled with restless tossing and turning, haunted by the faces of those he'd once trusted, now looking at him with a mixture of fear and calculation. The opulent penthouse suite, once a symbol of his success, now felt like a gilded cage, confining him to a world of paranoia and suspicion.

He spent his days in a whirlwind of legal maneuvers, his lawyer, Veronica, a ghost of her former self, moving with a cautious precision that bordered on detachment. Her reassurances were thin, her advice laced with a pragmatism that chilled him to the bone. He understood; self-preservation was a primal instinct, especially in this brutal game. Veronica was playing it safe, protecting her own interests, and he couldn't blame her. He had taught her that lesson, after all.

His phone buzzed incessantly, a relentless stream of calls from anxious investors, worried executives, and opportunistic vultures circling his empire like carrion birds. Each conversation chipped away at his resolve, the constant pressure eroding his confidence. The financial ramifications were staggering. His empire, built on a foundation of ambition and relentless drive, was teetering on the brink of collapse.

One evening, under the cloak of darkness, he met with Sal Demarco, a notorious fixer with connections that extended into the darkest corners of the city. Sal, a man whose reputation was as grimy as his tailored suits, operated in the shadows, a master puppeteer pulling strings in the city's underbelly. He was the kind of man Big D had once admired, even emulated in his rise to power. Now, he was desperate enough to seek his help.

The meeting took place in a dimly lit Italian restaurant, tucked away in a forgotten corner of the city, a place where hushed conversations and furtive glances were the norm. The air was thick with the aroma of garlic and the undercurrent of unspoken threats. Sal was all business, his words precise, devoid of any unnecessary pleasantries.

"So, Big D," Sal said, his voice a low rumble, "Serena's singing like a canary. The Feds are sniffing around, and your empire's looking a little shaky."

Big D met Sal's gaze, his own eyes unwavering. "I need this cleaned up, Sal. Discreetly. Before it all comes crashing down."

Sal leaned back, a glint of calculation in his eyes. "Discreetly comes with a price, my friend. A hefty one. And it's not just money. We're talking… influence. Favor. Certain… compromises."

The silence hung between them, heavy and charged. Big D knew what Sal was implying, knew the compromises would be morally questionable, perhaps even illegal. But desperation had a way of warping one's moral compass. The price of his ambition, he was realizing, was far steeper than he had ever imagined.

Sal outlined his plan, an intricate web of deception and manipulation, involving silenced witnesses, fabricated evidence, and a calculated campaign to discredit Serena. It was a dangerous gamble, a desperate play for survival, but Big D saw no other option. He had to fight, not only for his empire, but for his freedom.

The following weeks were a blur of clandestine meetings, whispered conversations, and frantic maneuvering. Big D played a dangerous game, balancing on the razor's edge between success and ruin. He used his vast network of contacts, his resources, and his ruthless determination to push back against the impending collapse. He pushed his lawyers, his accountants, his remaining loyal associates to the limit, demanding their utmost dedication, their absolute loyalty.

The moral dilemma gnawed at him. He was sacrificing his integrity, compromising his principles, all for the sake of preserving his empire. He was becoming the very thing he had once despised, a ruthless manipulator, willing to do anything to achieve his goals. The line between right and wrong blurred, replaced by a chilling pragmatism that dictated his every move.

One particular meeting with a disgruntled former employee, a man named Ray who held damaging information about Big D's past, was particularly harrowing. Ray was a volatile individual, prone to fits of rage, a man who harbored a deep resentment towards Big D. Big D had to navigate a minefield of threats and intimidation to get Ray to sign a non-disclosure agreement, a deal that involved a significant financial payoff and a promise of protection – promises he wasn't entirely sure he could keep.

As the investigation intensified, Big D found himself more isolated than ever. The loyalty of his team, once a source of strength, had crumbled under the pressure, replaced by a climate of fear and self-preservation. Even Marcus, his most trusted confidant, seemed to be growing distant, his unwavering loyalty wavering under the relentless pressure.

The gamble Sal Demarco had proposed was far more intricate and dangerous than he initially imagined, demanding every ounce of his cunning, every shred of his ruthless ambition. He was caught in a web of his own making, a desperate struggle for survival against the forces of the law and the betrayals of those he once considered friends.

The line between his ambition and his self-destruction blurred. He was fighting not just for his empire, but for the validation of a life built on risky choices, a life he feared would vanish, leaving him empty and exposed. Each risky move only drew him deeper into the mire, the consequences of his actions hanging heavy in the air, an ever-present reminder of the steep price he was paying for his ambition. The truth was slowly unraveling, exposing the dark secrets at the heart of his empire, forcing Big D to confront not just the wrath of the law but the emptiness of a success built on a foundation of betrayal and ruthlessness. The desperate gamble he'd taken was far from over, and the odds were stacked heavily against him.

The air in the courtroom hung thick with anticipation, a palpable tension that crackled between Big D and Serena. She sat across the room, a stark contrast to her glamorous stage persona. The makeup was minimal, her usual vibrant outfits replaced by a simple, somber grey suit. Yet, her eyes, usually sparkling with confidence and mischief, burned with a cold intensity that sent a shiver down Big D's spine. He'd underestimated her, underestimated the depth of her anger, the unwavering resolve in her gaze. He'd built his empire on calculated risks, but this… this felt different. This felt personal.

Veronica, his lawyer, leaned in, her voice a low whisper. "Remember the strategy. Deny everything. Let them prove it." Her words were a balm to his frayed nerves, a lifeline in the stormy sea of this legal battle. But even her practiced calm couldn't fully quell the rising tide of apprehension within him.

The prosecutor, a sharp, ambitious woman named Ms. Riley, began her cross-examination, her questions precise, deliberate, each one a carefully placed dart aimed at the heart of Big D's carefully constructed narrative. She started with the smaller details, probing inconsistencies in his financial records, questioning the legitimacy of certain deals, subtly painting a picture of a man who operated in the grey areas of the law, a man willing to bend the rules, and even break them, to achieve his goals.

Big D answered calmly, his voice measured, his responses carefully crafted, each word weighed, each pause calculated. He'd prepared for this, spent countless hours rehearsing his answers, anticipating the questions. Yet, there was a tremor in his voice, a subtle crack in his facade that he couldn't quite control. The pressure was immense, the weight of his empire, the potential loss of his freedom, pressing down on him. He felt the gaze of the jury on him, their judgment hanging heavy in the air.

Then, Ms. Riley shifted her focus. She turned to Serena's testimony, weaving together a narrative of manipulation, exploitation, and systematic control. She painted a picture of Big D as a ruthless predator, preying on vulnerable young artists, exploiting their dreams for his own gain. The evidence, meticulously presented, was damning. Contracts that favored Big D's company, financial transactions that were deliberately opaque, and testimonials from other artists who had worked with him, each one adding a layer to the devastating portrait she was building.

The courtroom was silent, the air thick with the weight of the accusations. Big D felt a cold sweat breaking out on his forehead. He glanced at Serena again. Her gaze was unwavering, a burning intensity that exposed the truth he had tried so hard to bury. The lies he'd spun, the carefully constructed facade of success, were crumbling before his eyes.

Ms. Riley's final question hit him like a punch to the gut. "Mr. Davis, did you or did you not coerce Ms. Jones into signing a contract that effectively stripped her of her artistic rights and a significant portion of her earnings?"

The question hung in the air, a stark challenge to Big D's carefully constructed narrative. He opened his mouth to answer, but the words wouldn't come. The truth, so long suppressed, clawed at the surface, threatening to expose the ugly reality behind his glittering empire.

He hesitated, the silence stretching, agonizingly long. The courtroom held its breath. Even Veronica seemed stunned by his hesitation. The weight of his actions, the consequences of his choices, crashed down on him with the force of a tidal wave. He saw Serena's face, her eyes reflecting years of suppressed pain, betrayal, and a quiet, simmering anger that resonated deep within him. He saw the faces of the other artists, their expressions mirroring her own.

Finally, he spoke, his voice barely a whisper. "Yes." The word hung in the air, a confession that shattered the carefully constructed illusion of his success. The room erupted in murmurs. The prosecution team exchanged glances of triumph. Serena's shoulders slumped slightly, as if a heavy burden had finally been lifted.

The revelation was a turning point, not just in the legal battle, but in Big D's own internal struggle. The years of deception, manipulation, and ruthlessness had taken their toll, eroding his soul, leaving him hollow and empty. The glittering façade of his success had been stripped away, exposing the raw, ugly truth beneath. He had built his empire on broken dreams and shattered trust.

The confrontation wasn't just a legal battle; it was a reckoning. It was a confrontation with his own past, with the choices he had made, and the man he had become. The weight of his actions pressed down on him, a crushing weight he could no longer ignore.

The following days were a blur of depositions, testimonies, and legal maneuvering. The once-impregnable walls of his empire crumbled under the weight of the truth. Investors pulled out, executives abandoned ship, his reputation in tatters. His lawyers scrambled to minimize the damage, to negotiate a plea bargain that could salvage something from the wreckage.

But Big D wasn't focused on the legal proceedings anymore. He was consumed by a different kind of battle, a battle with his own conscience. The weight of his past actions, the pain he had caused, consumed him. He was haunted by the faces of the artists he had exploited, their dreams crushed under the heel of his ambition.

He met Serena again, this time not in the sterile environment of a courtroom, but in a quiet, dimly lit café. There was no anger in her eyes, only a profound sadness, a weary acceptance. She spoke of her struggle, her years of hardship and exploitation, the toll it had taken on her mental and emotional health. Her words were a mirror reflecting the damage he had caused.

The encounter wasn't a reconciliation, not yet. But it was the beginning of a long, arduous process of healing, of atonement. Big D was left with the wreckage of his empire, the ruins of his reputation, and the crushing weight of his past actions. He had faced the music, and the music was harsh, unforgiving, a symphony of regret and self-reproach. He had to rebuild his life, not from the ashes of his empire, but from the ruins of his own soul. This was a battle far more challenging than any he had faced in the cutthroat world of the music industry. The road to redemption was long and arduous, but he knew, deep down, that it was the only path forward. The unraveling of the truth had led him to a crossroads, a point where he had to confront not just the legal consequences, but the moral bankruptcy that had fueled his rise. The consequences of his choices were far-reaching, touching not just his career but the lives of those he had hurt. And now, he had to face them, one by one. The fight for his freedom was over, but the fight for his soul had just begun.

## Chapter 3: Betrayal and Redemption

The courtroom's hushed silence following Big D's confession felt heavier than any verdict. It was a silence pregnant with unspoken accusations, shattered loyalties, and the chilling realization that the meticulously constructed façade of Big D's empire was nothing more than a house of cards, easily toppled by the wind of truth. The air, once thick with anticipation, now hung heavy with the stench of betrayal.

Outside the courtroom, the news spread like wildfire. The whispers turned into shouts, the murmurs into headlines screaming "Empire Crumbles!" and "Mogul's Confession Rocks Music World!". Big D's carefully cultivated image, built on years of shrewd maneuvering and calculated PR, shattered into a million pieces. His once-unwavering supporters began to distance themselves, their allegiances shifting with the winds of public opinion.

The fallout hit his inner circle first. Marcus, his right-hand man, a loyal friend since their days hustling on the streets, felt a deep sense of betrayal. He'd always believed in Big D, even through the morally ambiguous dealings that had built their empire. But Big D's admission in court had exposed a chasm between their values, a fundamental difference in their understanding of right and wrong that could no longer be ignored. The weight of the revelation pressed upon him, eroding the foundation of their decades-long friendship. He wrestled with his loyalty, torn between his past and a future clouded by doubt and disillusionment.

Meanwhile, Lisa, Big D's fiercely ambitious head of marketing, saw the crumbling empire as an opportunity, a chance to seize power in the chaos. Her loyalty was always transactional, tied to power and influence. Big D's fall offered her a chance to climb the ladder, to take his place at the helm. She discreetly began making contact with rival labels, subtly positioning herself for a takeover, even as she feigned loyalty and concern for her fallen boss. Her ambition, previously masked by professionalism, now revealed itself in a ruthless pursuit of power.

The junior employees, those who had bought into Big D's charm and the allure of his success, felt a sense of disillusionment, a crushing realization that the dreams they'd invested in were founded on deceit. The lavish offices, the expensive perks, the promises of a life of luxury, all felt tainted, poisoned by the knowledge of Big D's wrongdoing. Morale plummeted. Whispers and accusations spread like a virus, infecting every corner of the company, turning colleagues into suspicious rivals.

Even Veronica, Big D's unflappable lawyer, felt the tremor of the earthquake that shook his world. Despite her professional detachment, a flicker of disappointment crossed her face. She'd defended countless clients accused of various crimes, but Big D's case was different. It touched on a deeper level of personal disappointment, a realization that the man she'd been fiercely defending had betrayed not just the law, but something much more fundamental. It tested her belief in the justice system and her own professional integrity.

The ensuing weeks were a blur of legal battles, frantic negotiations, and the desperate attempts to salvage what remained of Big D's empire. His lawyers worked tirelessly, trying to minimize the damage, negotiating with investors and creditors, and fighting to protect what was left of his assets. But the damage was irreparable. The truth had seeped out like poison into every aspect of his life. The trust, once a cornerstone of his success, was gone, replaced by suspicion, distrust, and outright animosity.

Big D himself retreated, isolating himself from the chaos. The public humiliation, the betrayal by those he considered friends, the weight of his actions – it all pressed down on him, crushing his spirit. The once-invincible mogul, used to dictating terms, now found himself at the mercy of events, utterly powerless. The glittering façade of success, so carefully constructed, lay in ruins. He spent his days alone, wrestling with his conscience, facing the bitter truth of his actions. The silence in his opulent penthouse was louder than the roar of the city outside. He was a prisoner in his own gilded cage.

His relationship with his mother, a woman who had always believed in him, was deeply strained. She'd seen him rise from the streets, overcome adversity, and build a remarkable empire. The news of his confession and the subsequent downfall was a crushing blow, eroding the pride she'd always felt in her son. She struggled to reconcile the man she knew, the man who had sacrificed so much to provide for her, with the man revealed in the courtroom. The conversations were strained, filled with unspoken accusations and the silent weight of disappointment.

The betrayal extended beyond his professional life, seeping into his personal relationships. His wife, initially supportive despite the whispers and rumors, found herself struggling to reconcile the public image with the man she'd married. The reality of his actions challenged her belief in their relationship. She wavered between loyalty and a deep sense of betrayal.

Big D's story became a cautionary tale. It was a parable about ambition, about the intoxicating allure of power, and the devastating consequences of unchecked greed and moral compromise. His fall from grace was a spectacle for the world to watch, a stark reminder that the price of success could be far higher than anticipated. It served as a testament to the fragility of trust, the destructive nature of betrayal, and the long, arduous road to redemption. His legal battles would eventually fade into the background, but the consequences of his actions, the emotional wreckage, the shattered relationships, would continue to resonate long after the headlines vanished. The story of Big D was a reminder that even in the ruthless world of the music industry, where survival of the fittest was the unspoken rule, the human cost of ambition could be devastating, and the price of betrayal far greater than any amount of wealth or power could ever compensate. The journey ahead was daunting, full of uncertainty and the lingering weight of past mistakes. But the first step on his path to redemption had already begun.

The fluorescent lights of the courtroom hummed a monotonous

tune, a stark contrast to the cacophony of the music industry Big D had once commanded. His tailored suit, usually a symbol of power, now seemed to hang loosely on his frame, a reflection of the weight of the accusations pressing down on him. Veronica, his lawyer, a seasoned veteran of legal battles, leaned in, her voice a low murmur barely audible above the hum of the lights. "They're pushing hard on the money laundering charges," she whispered, her breath warm against his ear. "The prosecution has a mountain of evidence."

The evidence indeed was formidable. A meticulously constructed web of shell corporations, offshore accounts, and falsified invoices, all painstakingly uncovered by the relentless investigation. Each document presented was a hammer blow to

Big D's meticulously crafted reputation. He'd thought he was clever, operating in the shadows, but the feds had been watching, patiently waiting for the right moment to strike. He watched as the prosecutor, a sharp, ambitious woman with eyes like ice, presented evidence—bank statements, wire transfers, emails detailing transactions that clearly pointed to a systematic pattern of tax evasion and money laundering. Each piece of evidence felt like a personal betrayal, a reminder of his arrogance and recklessness.

The witness testimonies were even more damaging. Former associates, some motivated by revenge, others by immunity deals, painted a picture of a man far removed from the public image he'd cultivated. They spoke of intimidation tactics, threats, and a culture of fear that had permeated his company. One former employee, a nervous young man barely able to meet the prosecutor's gaze, described how he was forced to falsify financial documents, his voice trembling with a mixture of fear and regret. Another, a hardened veteran of the music industry, recounted Big D's ruthless tactics, his willingness to bend the rules – and break them – to achieve his goals. Their testimonies were devastating, chipping away at Big D's defense, piece by piece.

Veronica fought back with the tenacity of a cornered lioness. She challenged the credibility of witnesses, pointed out inconsistencies in their accounts, and attacked the validity of the evidence. She argued that the prosecution's case was based on circumstantial evidence and conjecture, that there was no direct proof of Big D's involvement in the illegal activities. She highlighted the complexities of the music industry's financial dealings, suggesting that many of the transactions were legitimate business practices, albeit perhaps poorly documented. She painted Big D as a victim of circumstance, a successful entrepreneur who'd fallen prey to unscrupulous associates and the aggressive tactics of ambitious prosecutors. But the prosecution was relentless, meticulously dismantling each point of her defense, providing counter-evidence and further corroborating witness testimony.

The pressure mounted. Days bled into weeks, each courtroom session a grueling battle of wits and wills. The weight of the accusations pressed down on Big D, a suffocating blanket of anxiety and self-doubt. Sleep became a luxury he could no longer afford, his nights filled with restless tossing and turning, haunted by the faces of those he had betrayed. His once-impeccable image was tarnished beyond repair; the media frenzy intensified with every new development in the case. The headlines screamed of his downfall, portraying him as a ruthless criminal, a fallen mogul whose empire was built on deceit and corruption.

The financial consequences were equally devastating. His assets were frozen, his investments threatened. His company, once a symbol of his success, now teetered on the brink of collapse. The threat of bankruptcy loomed large, and with it the specter of losing everything he had worked so hard to achieve. The lavish lifestyle he had come to expect was gone, replaced by a chilling reality of legal fees, potential prison time, and the utter devastation of his reputation.

During the breaks, Veronica would try to offer words of encouragement, but even her unflappable demeanor seemed strained, her optimism wearing thin. She confided in him that the prosecution's case was strong, that the odds were stacked against them. "They want a conviction," she said, her voice low, "and they're willing to do whatever it takes to get it." The realization hit Big D with the force of a physical blow. He'd always been used to controlling the narrative, to manipulating situations to his advantage. But in the cold, hard reality of the courtroom, he was powerless, completely at the mercy of the system he'd so often exploited.

The trial dragged on, each day a grueling ordeal. The courtroom became a battleground, the air thick with tension, the silence punctuated by the sharp exchanges between Veronica and the prosecutor. Big D sat impassively, his face a mask of controlled composure, hiding the turmoil raging within. He watched as his carefully constructed world crumbled around him, piece by piece, brick by brick. He'd built his empire on ambition, ruthlessness, and a disregard for the consequences of his actions. Now, he was paying the price.

The final day of the trial arrived like a looming storm. The jury filed into the courtroom, their faces impassive, their expressions offering no clue as to their verdict. Big D sat motionless, his heart pounding a frantic rhythm against his ribs. The tension in the courtroom was palpable, a suffocating silence broken only by the judge's clearing of his throat. The verdict was read, each word hanging in the air, heavy with consequence. Guilty. The word echoed through the courtroom, a chilling proclamation that marked the end of one chapter and the beginning of another. The weight of his actions, the betrayal, the fall from grace—it was all now undeniable. The road to redemption would be long and arduous, a journey filled with challenges and uncertainties. But for now, he had to face the consequences of his actions, the price he would inevitably pay for the life he'd built on broken promises and shattered dreams. The battle was far from over.

The cold steel of the prison bars felt strangely familiar, a chilling echo of the iron grip he'd held on his empire. The harsh fluorescent lights, a constant reminder of the courtroom's sterile judgment, were replaced by the dim, flickering bulbs of his cell. The silence, once broken only by the rhythmic tapping of Veronica's heels on the courtroom floor, was now filled with the distant sounds of shouting, the clanking of metal, and the unsettling quiet of men wrestling with their own demons.

Big D, stripped of his tailored suits and designer clothes, was reduced to the simple, drab uniform of an inmate. The expensive cologne he'd favored was replaced by the pungent odor of sweat, stale air, and despair. The weight of his conviction pressed down on him, not just as a legal sentence, but as a crushing burden of guilt. The meticulously crafted image he'd spent years building, the persona of a self-made mogul, a symbol of success against all odds, was shattered. Now, he was just a number, a statistic, a convicted criminal.

The initial shock of the verdict gave way to a slow, agonizing wave of introspection. He stared at the peeling paint on the wall, his mind racing, replaying the events that had led him here. The relentless pursuit of success, the willingness to bend rules, the blind ambition that had consumed him – all of it came crashing down. The faces of those he'd betrayed flashed before his eyes: Serena, her accusations ringing in his ears; his former associates, their resentful faces a testament to his ruthless tactics; his mother, her disappointed gaze a constant ache in his heart. He'd hurt so many people, and for what? A fleeting sense of power, a hollow achievement that had ultimately led to his downfall.

He thought of the countless hours he'd dedicated to building his empire, the risks he'd taken, the sacrifices he'd made. He'd risen from the poverty-stricken streets of Chicago, clawing his way to the top, fueled by ambition and a fierce determination to escape the cycle of hardship that had defined his early life. But in his relentless ascent, he'd lost sight of his values, his morals, his humanity. He'd become a product of the very system he'd sought to conquer.

The harsh reality of his situation forced him to confront his past, not just the illegal activities that had led to his conviction, but the deeper flaws within his character. He'd been driven by an insatiable hunger for power, a need for validation that bordered on obsession. He'd treated people as pawns, expendable pieces in his game of ambition. He'd manipulated, intimidated, and exploited those around him without remorse. His success had come at a terrible cost, a cost he was now forced to pay.

The prison library became his sanctuary, a refuge from the harsh reality of his surroundings. He delved into books, seeking solace and knowledge. He read philosophy, searching for answers, for a way to understand his own motivations and reconcile his past actions. He read history, studying the rise and fall of empires, the lessons learned from the mistakes of others. He devoured literature, immersing himself in the stories of redemption, the possibility of change.

The initial bitterness and resentment gradually gave way to a grudging acceptance of responsibility. He spent hours writing in a worn notebook, pouring out his thoughts, his regrets, his hopes for the future. The act of writing became a form of therapy, a way to process his emotions, to confront his demons, to begin the arduous journey of self-improvement. He started with simple reflections, chronicling his days, his feelings, his struggles. Then, he began to explore the roots of his actions, delving deeper into the psychological factors that had driven his behavior. He acknowledged his flaws, his arrogance, his ruthlessness, his lack of empathy. He accepted that he was not a victim, but a perpetrator, fully accountable for his choices.

He started to engage in the prison programs, initially out of a sense of obligation, but gradually finding a sense of purpose in his involvement. He participated in anger management workshops, learning to control his impulsive nature. He joined a literacy program, helping others learn to read and write, finding a strange sense of satisfaction in sharing his own hard-won knowledge. He even participated in a restorative justice program, reaching out to those he'd harmed, seeking forgiveness and attempting to make amends.

One particular encounter stood out. He wrote a letter to Serena, a letter not of apology, but of genuine remorse. He didn't try to justify his actions or minimize his wrongdoing. He simply acknowledged the pain he'd caused and expressed his deep regret. He didn't expect forgiveness, but he hoped that his letter might offer some measure of closure. He received a response, a short, simple letter, but one that carried a weight of profound significance. Serena's words offered a glimmer of hope, a hint that his efforts at redemption might not be in vain.

The road to redemption wasn't easy. There were setbacks, moments of doubt, temptations to fall back into old habits. He faced hostility from other inmates, the constant reminder of his past, the judgment in their eyes. But he persevered, fueled by a growing sense of purpose, a commitment to change that stemmed from deep within. He continued to write, reflecting on his experiences, learning from his mistakes, charting his progress. He found a sense of peace in helping others, in contributing to the community within the prison walls. He discovered a strength within himself, a resilience he hadn't known he possessed.

His transformation wasn't dramatic, nor was it instantaneous. It was a slow, gradual process, a continuous struggle against his own impulses and the ingrained habits of a lifetime. But it was real, and it was tangible. He was no longer the same man who had entered those prison walls. The ambition that had once consumed him was now channeled into self-improvement, into a desire to make amends for his past. The ruthlessness he'd once embraced had been replaced by empathy and a genuine concern for others. The man who had once reveled in power now found solace in humility and the quiet dignity of hard-won self-respect.

The possibility of parole loomed, a beacon of hope in the distance. He knew the journey wouldn't end there; redemption would be a lifelong process, a continuous struggle against his inner demons. But as he prepared to face the outside world, he was no longer filled with fear or anxiety. He carried the weight of his past, but he also carried the strength of his transformation, a newfound purpose, and a quiet hope for a future that would be defined not by ambition or ruthlessness but by integrity, compassion, and a genuine desire to make a positive impact on the world. The music industry, once a symbol of his downfall, might no longer be his stage. But he had found a new kind of rhythm in his life, a cadence of self-reflection, and an enduring commitment to making amends for his past, one day, one step, one word at a time.

The prison walls, once a symbol of his isolation, now felt strangely porous. The rigid structure of incarceration, designed to separate, had inadvertently created a space for unexpected connections. It started subtly, with shared glances across the mess hall, a brief nod of acknowledgement during yard time, a quiet exchange of words during a particularly brutal thunderstorm that rattled the aging building. These small gestures, initially hesitant and guarded, gradually blossomed into something more profound.

One of the most unexpected connections was with Carlos, a wiry, aging man serving time for a crime he vehemently maintained he didn't commit. Carlos, a former accountant with a sharp mind and an even sharper tongue, had initially treated Big D with the same disdain most inmates reserved for a former mogul. But Big D's quiet demeanor, his genuine engagement in prison programs, and his willingness to help others—even those who openly resented his presence—gradually chipped away at Carlos's cynicism.

Carlos, a master of financial intricacies, saw a shrewd mind behind Big D's hardened exterior. They spent hours in the library, poring over legal texts, debating legal strategies, and analyzing the flaws in the case that landed Big D behind bars. Carlos's skepticism transformed into a grudging respect, eventually into a form of begrudging friendship. He was surprisingly adept at explaining the complexities of the legal system, providing Big D with a newfound understanding of the machinations that had led to his conviction.

Their alliance wasn't forged in mutual gain but in a shared desire for justice and a surprising understanding of each other's vulnerabilities. Carlos, despite his claims of innocence, carried a deep-seated sorrow, a shadow of regret that resonated with Big D's own self-recriminations. They found solace in their shared adversity, their conversations evolving beyond legal strategy into philosophical discussions about the nature of justice, morality, and the enduring power of the human spirit. They dissected the lives they'd led, exploring the choices that had brought them to this desolate place, acknowledging the consequences, and searching for meaning amidst the chaos.

Another unlikely ally emerged in the person of Marcus, a young man serving time for a drug-related offense. Marcus, initially resentful of Big D's wealth and privilege, saw in Big D's commitment to the prison's literacy program a genuine desire to help others. Big D patiently worked with Marcus, helping him improve his reading and writing skills. Marcus's past was marred by violence and instability, a stark contrast to Big D's calculated ambition. Yet, they found common ground in their shared experiences of hardship and struggle, their conversations revealing the underlying vulnerabilities beneath their hardened exteriors. Marcus helped Big D understand the street life that he'd once only superficially observed, providing insights into the systemic issues that contribute to crime and poverty. Big D, in turn, shared his business acumen, helping Marcus develop a plan for his future, offering him hope and a path towards a life free from violence and addiction.

These alliances weren't solely defined by personal connections but expanded to include other inmates. Big D's reputation, initially one of fear and intimidation, began to shift. He was no longer seen merely as a fallen mogul but as a man who was actively working to overcome his past and make amends. He helped other inmates with their legal paperwork, aided in composing letters to their families, and became a quiet leader within the prison community, fostering a sense of unity and camaraderie amongst those who were often alienated and marginalized.

The transformation wasn't swift or spectacular, but it was undeniable. The prison, a place designed to dehumanize, became a crucible where Big D, Carlos, and Marcus, forged a bond of mutual respect and understanding, challenging the very nature of their confinement. Their alliance transcended the confines of the prison walls. They began to reach out beyond the institution, utilizing their newfound connections to support those still caught in the cycle of poverty and crime. This outreach extended to Big D's former business associates, many of whom had distanced themselves from him following his conviction. Some, still harboring resentment, remained skeptical. Others, however, recognizing his genuine remorse and the transformative changes he had undergone, began to offer support and cooperation, acknowledging the strength of his transformation.

The unexpected alliances, built on shared adversity and a commitment to change, demonstrated a powerful force for redemption. It wasn't merely about forgiveness; it was about understanding, about acknowledging shared human experiences, and about finding strength in unity amidst adversity. The prison had become an unlikely incubator for collaboration and resilience, challenging the notion that individuals are defined solely by their past actions. Big D's journey toward redemption was now inextricably linked to these unlikely friendships, highlighting the human capacity for growth, forgiveness, and the potential for transformative change even within the confines of a correctional facility.

Serena's letter, a single sheet of paper bearing a brief message of understanding, became a catalyst for this profound shift. While not explicitly forgiving, it implicitly acknowledged Big D's sincere efforts toward self-improvement. This subtle acceptance gave weight to the changes he had made, bolstering the sense of purpose he had found within the prison walls. Her letter was not just a message of personal reconciliation but a symbol of hope, a recognition that redemption was possible, even in the face of immense betrayal. The fact that she had acknowledged his efforts resonated deeply with Big D, validating his transformation and serving as a powerful impetus to further his work toward making amends for his past actions.

The unexpected alliances solidified Big D's commitment to genuine change. He realized that his redemption wasn't simply a personal journey but a responsibility extending to those he had wronged. He began to actively seek ways to make restitution for his actions, not just through legal processes, but by addressing the underlying social and economic issues that contributed to his own rise and fall. This broadened perspective shifted his focus from personal gain to collective responsibility, transforming him into a catalyst for social change, albeit on a smaller, more localized scale.

The network of support he cultivated within the prison walls extended beyond the inmates to involve prison staff and community outreach programs. He leveraged his business acumen to help inmates secure employment opportunities upon release, bridging the gap between incarceration and reintegration. He worked with social workers to develop programs aimed at reducing recidivism and assisting former inmates in accessing essential resources like housing and job training. These initiatives were not grand gestures of philanthropy but meticulously planned and executed strategies built on his newfound understanding of the systemic issues that perpetuate cycles of poverty and crime.

Big D's journey from powerful record executive to incarcerated individual and then, ultimately, to a champion for social justice, was a testament to the enduring human capacity for growth and transformation. The unexpected alliances forged within the confines of prison walls became the cornerstones of his redemption, showcasing the surprising power of unity and empathy, even in the most challenging circumstances. The unexpected alliances weren't just about escaping the confines of prison; they were about breaking free from the limitations of the past and embracing a future defined by responsibility, compassion, and genuine commitment to making amends, not just to those he personally harmed, but to a larger society that he had previously manipulated and exploited. The cold steel of the bars no longer felt like a barrier but a crucible in which a new self was forged, stronger, more empathetic, and determined to create positive change. His story was no longer one of a self-made mogul's downfall but a testament to the power of human resilience and the transformative potential of unexpected alliances.

The courtroom doors swung shut behind him, the metallic clang echoing the finality of his sentence. But the silence that followed wasn't the suffocating quiet of defeat. It was a pregnant stillness, heavy with the weight of the future, a future he was determined to shape differently. The initial shock of incarceration had given way to a steely resolve. His empire, once a symbol of his ambition, lay in ruins, a testament to his hubris and the betrayals he'd suffered. Yet, amidst the wreckage, a new foundation was being laid.

The prison wasn't the tomb he'd initially envisioned. It was a crucible, a harsh and unforgiving environment that stripped away the superficiality and forced a brutal honesty. The shared hardship fostered unexpected alliances, forging connections that transcended the bars and the ingrained prejudices of the outside world. Carlos, the cynical accountant, became a trusted confidante, his legal expertise proving invaluable in navigating the complexities of his appeal process. Marcus, the young man grappling with addiction, found in Big D a mentor, a quiet leader who helped him build a future far removed from the streets.

Their collaboration extended beyond the prison walls. Carlos, utilizing his network of contacts, began discreetly rebuilding Big D's financial infrastructure, piecing together salvaged assets and exploring new investment opportunities. He was more than an advisor; he was a partner, a silent force working to restore Big D's standing, not for personal gain, but out of respect for the man he'd come to know. This meticulous work laid the groundwork for a new venture, one born not from the relentless pursuit of wealth but from a desire to create something meaningful and lasting.

The literacy program Big D championed within the prison walls became a catalyst for his own personal growth. He'd always been a man of action, a builder, but the quiet act of teaching, of patiently guiding others toward knowledge and self-improvement, revealed a depth he'd previously overlooked. He discovered a passion for education, a desire to provide opportunities to those who lacked access, a commitment that extended far beyond the prison walls.

Upon his release, a process shrouded in legal maneuvering and tense negotiations, Big D found himself transformed. The brash, ambitious mogul was gone, replaced by a man marked by humility and a fierce determination to rebuild, not just his business, but his life and reputation. His vision for the future was no longer focused solely on the dizzying heights of success in the music industry. Instead, he envisioned a future built on ethical principles, a future where his business model incorporated social responsibility and community investment.

The record label, resurrected with careful planning and strategic partnerships, became a vehicle for social change. It focused on signing and promoting artists from underserved communities, providing them with opportunities for mentorship, education, and financial literacy. Big D understood the systemic inequalities that had shaped his own rise and fall, and he was determined to use his experience and resources to address them. This new business model wasn't simply about profit; it was about creating a sustainable ecosystem of support, one that nourished artistic talent while simultaneously addressing the social and economic challenges facing the communities from which his artists emerged.

His relationships, too, were redefined. His family, initially estranged by his ambition and the ensuing scandal, gradually forgave him. His mother, his bedrock, saw the genuine remorse in his actions. She understood the depths of his regret and embraced the changed man he had become. His interactions with Serena were marked by a profound respect and a shared understanding of the hurt and betrayal they'd both endured. While forgiveness wasn't easily granted, there was a quiet acknowledgement of the pain and a shared commitment to healing. The relationship wasn't necessarily restored to its previous level, but it became a foundation of mutual respect, reflecting a maturity and understanding that had been absent before.

Big D's journey was not simply a personal redemption arc; it was a transformation that ripple-effected the lives of those around him. Marcus, inspired by Big D's commitment to education and social justice, secured a position with a non-profit organization dedicated to youth outreach programs. His past struggles, far from defining him, became a driving force in his work. He became an advocate for those who had experienced similar challenges, his life a testament to the resilience of the human spirit.

Carlos, having played a crucial role in rebuilding Big D's business, continued to mentor him, providing sage advice and unwavering support. Their relationship went beyond that of a business partnership; it evolved into a deep-rooted friendship. They met regularly, not just to discuss finances but to share insights about their journeys, their triumphs and failures. They remained allies, their common experience creating an unshakeable bond that transcended their personal goals. Their unlikely partnership, forged in the crucible of adversity, became a model for the collaboration and mutual support that defined Big D's new business approach.

The new Big D was not merely a reformed man; he was an advocate for social justice. He established a foundation dedicated to providing educational and vocational training to underprivileged youth, mirroring the programs he'd developed within the prison walls. This outreach extended beyond his immediate network to include community initiatives aimed at breaking the cycle of poverty and crime. His business became a model for ethical business practice, integrating social responsibility into every aspect of its operations. He leveraged his influence and resources to support organizations working to address systemic inequalities, proving that success could be redefined as something far more substantial than simply accumulating wealth.

The scars of his past remained, etched indelibly into his life, but they served as reminders of his journey, not impediments to his future. The legal battles, the betrayals, the imprisonment – these were not chapters to be erased from his story but essential elements that formed the narrative of his transformation. He acknowledged his past mistakes, not with self-pity but with a determined resolve to make amends and to create a lasting positive impact.

His story became one of resilience, transformation, and the unexpected power of second chances. It was a narrative woven not just with the threads of ambition and success, but with the strength of compassion, the unwavering commitment to social justice, and the remarkable capacity of the human spirit to overcome adversity. The journey from self-made mogul to incarcerated individual and finally, to a champion for social change, was a testament to the potential for growth and redemption, even in the darkest of circumstances. The aftermath of his downfall wasn't simply a rebuilding of an empire; it was a metamorphosis that reshaped his life, his values, and the world around him, proving that even amidst betrayal and devastating consequences, a new beginning is possible, fueled by resilience, understanding, and a genuine commitment to making amends.

## Chapter 4: Consequences and Reckoning

The courtroom was thick with anticipation, a suffocating silence broken only by the rhythmic ticking of the grandfather clock in the corner. Big D sat ramrod straight, his usual swagger replaced by a controlled stillness. He'd spent weeks poring over legal documents with Carlos, meticulously crafting a defense strategy that acknowledged his mistakes while highlighting the manipulative tactics employed by Serena and others within his organization. The prosecution, however, had painted a damning picture, skillfully weaving a narrative of greed, corruption, and blatant disregard for the law.

The jury's deliberation felt like an eternity, each tick of the clock amplifying the tension. When the foreman finally announced the verdict, it was a mixture of relief and a bitter sting. Big D was found guilty on several counts, including tax evasion and obstruction of justice, but acquitted on the more serious charges of fraud and conspiracy. The sentence: five years, a significant term, yet far less than the potentially ruinous twenty years the prosecution had sought. The weight of the gavel's fall was palpable, a finality that settled over the courtroom like a shroud.

The verdict, while not a complete victory, felt like a reprieve. It was a testament to the diligence of Carlos and the strength of the defense's strategy. More importantly, it provided a path forward, a chance to rebuild, even if from a foundation of ashes. But the victory was bittersweet. The shadow of the conviction would forever loom large, a stain on his previously untarnished reputation. The media frenzy that followed was predictable and relentless. The headlines screamed of his downfall, a cautionary tale of ambition gone awry.

Serena, though initially triumphant, found the aftermath more complicated than anticipated. The trial had exposed her own questionable dealings, her past manipulations laid bare for all to see. While she'd achieved her goal of bringing Big D down, she found herself ostracized by much of the industry. Her career, once soaring, now teetered on the brink of collapse, tarnished by her association with the scandal and the revelation of her own less-than-ethical practices. The victory felt hollow, a pyrrhic win that cost her far more than she'd anticipated.

For Marcus, the verdict brought a wave of mixed emotions. He felt a sense of justice served, yet also a profound sadness. Big D, despite his flaws, had been a mentor, a figure who'd shown him a path away from the destructive cycle of street life. He witnessed the man's remorse, his genuine efforts at self-improvement during his imprisonment, and the subsequent transformation he underwent. This made it difficult to see Big D solely as the villain the media portrayed. This internal conflict drove him further towards his work with the youth outreach programs, determined to break cycles of crime and despair for others.

Carlos, ever the pragmatist, immediately shifted his focus to mitigating the fallout of the conviction. He began to salvage what remained of Big D's assets, negotiating with creditors and exploring avenues for rebuilding the record label from the ground up. He knew the road ahead would be long and arduous, but he was unwavering in his commitment to helping Big D navigate the complex legal and financial challenges that lay ahead. Their relationship, already strong, was solidified by their shared experience and a mutual commitment to securing a positive future.

The five years Big D spent in prison were a crucible, refining his character and challenging his core beliefs. The initial shock gave way to a quiet introspection, and the harsh realities of prison life forced him to confront his past actions. It wasn't just the deprivation and the daily struggle for survival, but also the profound loneliness that gnawed at him. He found solace in unexpected places: the quiet dignity of an elderly inmate who shared his love of literature, the shared grief of a young father separated from his family, the unspoken camaraderie built among men united by hardship.

The prison's literacy program became a lifeline, a way to escape the bleak reality of his surroundings and connect with something larger than himself. He discovered a talent for teaching, a patience he never knew he possessed. His lessons extended beyond the basics of reading and writing, becoming discussions about life, morality, and the power of self-improvement. He mentored other inmates, guiding them towards self-discovery and helping them plan their futures.

His time in prison wasn't a period of passive suffering; it was a period of active transformation. He began to examine his past, not with self-pity or bitterness, but with a raw honesty and a determination to learn from his mistakes. He found a new understanding of justice, a concept that extended beyond the courtroom and into the realm of personal accountability. This newfound understanding fundamentally reshaped his perspective on wealth, success, and social responsibility.

Upon his release, Big D was a changed man. The brash, self-assured mogul was gone, replaced by a man humbled by adversity and determined to make amends. The media still followed his every move, but now their focus shifted from his scandalous past to his unwavering efforts at rehabilitation. His commitment to positive social change, fueled by his experiences and his genuine remorse, became a powerful narrative, one that slowly began to eclipse the negative publicity.

The resurrected record label became a reflection of his transformed values. It was no longer simply about finding the next big star; it was about empowering artists from disadvantaged backgrounds, fostering creativity within a supportive environment, and nurturing their development as both musicians and responsible members of their communities. The company invested in education, job training, and mentorship, ensuring that the artists on its roster had access to opportunities they might not otherwise have had. It was a business built on sustainability and social justice, a stark contrast to the ruthlessly ambitious enterprise of his earlier years.

His relationship with his family was slowly repaired. His mother, ever supportive, saw the change in him, the genuine contrition, and the quiet commitment to living a life of integrity. While forgiveness took time, their bond, strengthened by shared experience, became even deeper than before. His relationship with Serena evolved as well, moving from animosity to a grudging respect. Neither one could erase the pain inflicted, but they both acknowledged their own roles in the unraveling of their previously close professional relationship.

Big D's story became a compelling narrative of redemption, not just for himself, but for others. His journey inspired many, proving that even amidst the darkest of circumstances, there is always the potential for growth, change, and a second chance. The legal battle, the prison sentence, the media onslaught — these were not just setbacks but vital elements of his transformation, shaping the man he became and influencing the positive change he brought about in the lives of others. He became a beacon of hope, demonstrating that even from the ruins of ambition and self-destruction, it's possible to build a life founded on integrity, compassion, and a profound commitment to making amends. His legacy wouldn't be solely defined by his past mistakes, but by his unwavering commitment to a future built on redemption and social responsibility. The justice served wasn't just the legal verdict; it was the transformative justice he brought about in his own life and the lives of those he touched.

The prison gates swung open, a clang of metal echoing the finality of his sentence. Freedom, however, felt less like liberation and more like a stark, uncertain landscape. The five years had reshaped him, etched lines of weariness onto his face, replaced the swagger with a quiet gravity. He was no longer Big D, the ruthless mogul. He was just D, a man stripped bare, facing the daunting task of rebuilding a life shattered by his own ambition.

The first few weeks were a disorienting blur. The cacophony of city sounds, the relentless rush of traffic, the sheer volume of human interaction—all of it felt overwhelming after the structured silence of prison. He'd envisioned a triumphant return, a comeback story worthy of the headlines. Instead, he felt lost, adrift in a world that had moved on without him. The media, ever-hungry for a spectacle, initially focused on his release, but the narrative lacked the sensationalism they craved. His story, stripped of its dramatic elements, was a quiet one, a slow, arduous process of rehabilitation and amends.

His mother's embrace was the first genuine comfort he received. Her eyes, though filled with a mixture of relief and sorrow, held an unwavering love. There were no grand pronouncements, no lectures on his failings. Just the quiet warmth of acceptance, a tacit understanding of the profound changes that had taken place within him. Their home, once a symbol of his success, now felt small and humble, a fitting backdrop to his new, simpler life.

His relationship with Marcus, however, proved more complex. Marcus, now a successful youth worker, saw Big D's release with a mixture of cautious optimism and lingering resentment. The years hadn't erased the hurt caused by Big D's past actions, particularly the impact on Marcus's own community. While acknowledging Big D's transformation, Marcus held him accountable for the damage he had inflicted. Their conversations were hesitant, punctuated by silences filled with unspoken grievances and the lingering weight of shared history. Slowly, however, a fragile bridge began to form, built not on forgiveness, but on a mutual commitment to the betterment of their community.

Carlos, ever practical, had been meticulously preparing for Big D's return. He'd managed to salvage a portion of the record label, restructuring the business to reflect Big D's newfound values. Gone was the relentless pursuit of profit at any cost; in its place was a commitment to ethical practices, social responsibility, and artist empowerment. The label, smaller and leaner, was a testament to Carlos's loyalty and unwavering belief in Big D's capacity for redemption.

The rebuilding of his professional life was a daunting task. His reputation was in tatters, trust eroded, and his network of contacts severely diminished. The industry, once his domain, now viewed him with a mixture of suspicion and curiosity. Yet, Big D's commitment to change proved contagious. The artists he signed, primarily from marginalized communities, were drawn to his authenticity, his humility, and his genuine desire to provide them with the resources and support they needed.

His new approach wasn't simply about producing hit records; it was about fostering a sense of community, providing mentorship, and promoting social justice. He established partnerships with local schools and community centers, offering educational and job training programs to young people. He became a vocal advocate for criminal justice reform, sharing his experiences to promote understanding and compassion. His story, once a cautionary tale of ambition gone awry, became an example of redemption, inspiring those who had previously dismissed him.

The media, initially hesitant, eventually shifted their narrative. The focus transitioned from sensationalized exposés to in-depth profiles highlighting Big D's efforts at rehabilitation and his commitment to social change. He found himself fielding interview requests from publications he'd once shunned, his words carrying a weight far different than the arrogant pronouncements of his past. His remorse was genuine, evident in his actions, his words, and the unwavering support of those he had once wronged and now sought to help.

His relationship with Serena remained complicated. The legal battle had left scars on both of them, a legacy of broken trust and bitter resentments. Yet, over time, a grudging respect evolved, a recognition of their shared mistakes and their individual journeys towards accountability. They never fully reconciled, but the mutual understanding they reached provided some measure of closure.

The five years in prison hadn't simply been a punishment; they'd been a crucible. The hardship, the introspection, the unwavering support of unexpected allies had forged a resilience and a humility he hadn't known he possessed. He emerged not unscathed but transformed. The weight of his past actions remained a constant reminder of the consequences of his choices. However, he carried that weight with a newfound dignity, a quiet determination to build a life defined not by the mistakes he had made, but by the amends he was making.

His story wasn't one of a miraculous, instantaneous transformation, but a slow, steady progression towards redemption. It wasn't easy; the challenges, both personal and professional, were relentless. Yet, his unwavering commitment to change, his genuine remorse, and the support of those who believed in him paved the way for a future built on integrity, compassion, and a profound commitment to making amends. His success wasn't measured in monetary terms, but in the lives he touched, the communities he helped, and the positive impact he had on the world. The justice he sought, he found not in the courtroom, but in the quiet, transformative power of his own redemption. He had paid his debt to society, but more importantly, he was paying the debt he owed to himself and those whose lives he'd irrevocably affected. The weight of the past remained, but it was a weight he carried with grace and a renewed purpose. His story became a testament to the enduring power of self-reflection, the possibility of transformation, and the unwavering belief in the capacity for second chances.

The first step was the hardest. It wasn't the physical act of walking out of prison, nor the initial shock of re-entering society, but the internal struggle to reconcile the man he'd been with the man he desperately wanted to become. He'd spent years building an empire on ambition, ruthlessness, and a disregard for the consequences of his actions. Now, he had to dismantle that empire, brick by agonizing brick, and rebuild it on a foundation of integrity and compassion.

His days were meticulously structured, a stark contrast to the chaotic life he'd once led. Mornings were dedicated to community service, volunteering at a local youth center, working with at-risk teenagers who reminded him of his younger self—lost, angry, and searching for a way out. He found himself relating to their struggles, not from a position of authority, but from a place of shared experience. He saw their potential, the untapped talent and ambition that had once burned within him but had been twisted and corrupted by circumstance and his own flawed judgment.

The afternoons were spent at Carlos's revamped record label. The office was smaller, the atmosphere far less frenetic. Gone were the ostentatious displays of wealth, the constant pressure to chase the next big hit. Instead, there was a quiet focus on nurturing talent, providing mentorship, and fostering a sense of collaboration. Carlos, ever the pragmatist, had streamlined the operation, cutting unnecessary expenses and emphasizing ethical practices. He had saved what he could, protecting not just the business, but Big D's legacy. Big D found solace in this new environment, a sense of purpose he'd been missing for years.

The evenings were for reflection. He devoured books on self-improvement, leadership, and social justice. He attended support groups, sharing his experiences, not seeking pity, but offering guidance to others battling their own demons. He started journaling, chronicling his journey, pouring his thoughts and emotions onto paper, a form of catharsis, a way to confront the ghosts of his past. The process was painful, exposing his vulnerabilities, forcing him to confront the darkness within, but it was necessary for his healing.

His relationship with Marcus remained delicate. Marcus didn't offer forgiveness easily; it was a process, a gradual thawing of resentment earned over years of betrayal. Marcus had seen firsthand the damage Big D's actions had caused within their community, and trust couldn't be instantly restored. Their conversations, initially stilted and uncomfortable, gradually grew deeper. They began to discuss their shared history, addressing the pain and hurt, not to dwell on the past, but to confront it, understand it, and learn from it. Big D listened intently, absorbing Marcus's criticisms, acknowledging his failures, and offering genuine remorse.

He made a conscious effort to repair the damage he had caused. He reached out to former business associates he had wronged, offering apologies and making amends wherever possible. Some were receptive, others remained skeptical. He accepted the rejection without bitterness, understanding that some wounds run too deep to be so easily healed. He learned that redemption is not about seeking forgiveness, but about earning it through consistent action and unwavering commitment to positive change.

The legal battles continued, but their focus shifted. The initial accusations had been sensationalized, fueled by media frenzy and personal vendettas. Now, the proceedings were more subdued, the narrative focused not on Big D's crimes but on his subsequent efforts at rehabilitation. His lawyers worked tirelessly to present his transformed self, a man committed to making amends and rebuilding his life on a moral foundation. The process was arduous, but Big D remained resolute, his commitment to change unshakeable.

The music industry, initially hesitant to embrace him, slowly started to accept his new approach. He signed artists who had been previously overlooked, promising them mentorship, support, and a fairer share of the profits. He emphasized artistic integrity over commercial success, prioritizing quality over quantity. He established workshops and training programs for aspiring musicians, providing them with opportunities they wouldn't otherwise have had. His label became a haven for artists from marginalized communities, a space where their voices could be heard and amplified.

He became a vocal advocate for criminal justice reform, leveraging his experience to shed light on the flaws within the system. He spoke at conferences, shared his story with legislators, and used his platform to promote meaningful change. He understood that his redemption was not only about his own personal transformation, but about contributing to a larger cause, using his influence to create positive social impact.

The media, initially preoccupied with the sensationalism of his downfall, eventually shifted their focus. In-depth profiles highlighting his rehabilitation and community involvement replaced the salacious headlines. He started receiving invitations to speak at universities, community forums, and even corporate events, a testament to the powerful narrative of his redemption.

Serena's presence remained a complex factor. The legal proceedings had frayed their relationship beyond repair, leaving them both scarred. Yet, over time, a grudging respect emerged. They had both made mistakes, inflicted pain, and endured the harsh consequences. They never became friends, but they reached a fragile understanding, acknowledging each other's journeys toward accountability and recognizing the shared responsibility for the damage inflicted. This unspoken truce provided a measure of closure.

His story wasn't a fairy tale of instant transformation. It wasn't a smooth, uninterrupted path to redemption. There were setbacks, moments of doubt, and temptations to revert to old habits. But each time, he found the strength to persevere, to recommit to his path of self-improvement, driven by a deep desire for genuine change.

The weight of his past actions never entirely disappeared, but it no longer crushed him. He learned to carry it with a newfound dignity and purpose. He understood that redemption is not about erasing the past but about learning from it, making amends, and striving to become a better person. His success wasn't measured in financial terms but in the positive impact he had on the lives of others, the communities he uplifted, and the systemic changes he helped bring about.

Big D's story became a testament to the enduring power of self-reflection, the transformative potential of adversity, and the importance of second chances. It's a story of a man who fell, but who had the courage to rise again, not as the ruthless mogul he once was, but as someone committed to making a positive difference in the world. He paid his debt to society, but more importantly, he paid the debt he owed himself, a debt of atonement, a debt fulfilled not through grand gestures, but through consistent action, humility, and an unwavering commitment to redemption. His journey was far from over, but the path he had chosen, however arduous, was finally leading him toward a future defined by hope, integrity, and purpose.

The courtroom doors closed behind her, a finality that resonated deeper than the gavel's thud. The legal battles were over, but the war within Serena raged on. The victory felt hollow, a pyrrhic win that had left her emotionally drained and spiritually wounded. The public narrative painted her as a brave whistleblower, a champion of justice, but the truth was far more nuanced, far more complicated. She hadn't emerged unscathed; the experience had stripped her bare, revealing vulnerabilities she hadn't known she possessed.

The initial euphoria of exposing Big D's misdeeds gave way to a profound sense of loneliness. The celebratory phone calls dwindled, the media frenzy subsided, leaving her adrift in a sea of silence. The support system she'd counted on, the network of allies and advocates who had rallied to her side, gradually dispersed, their attention shifting to other causes, other narratives. She was left to confront the aftermath alone, grappling with the emotional fallout, the lingering trauma, and the uncertainty of her future.

Her apartment, once a vibrant hub of activity, felt cold and empty. The walls, once adorned with celebratory posters and awards, seemed to mock her with their silent judgment. Sleep offered little respite; nightmares plagued her, haunting visions of the courtroom, the intense interrogation, the relentless pressure. She sought therapy, pouring her heart out to a stranger, someone who wouldn't judge her, someone who could help her navigate the treacherous terrain of her emotional landscape.

Therapy became her sanctuary, a space where she could unravel the tangled threads of her past, confronting the trauma she had suppressed for so long. The process was agonizing, forcing her to confront the deep-seated insecurities that had made her vulnerable to manipulation and exploitation. She learned to identify the warning signs, to recognize the patterns of abuse, and to develop the tools she needed to protect herself from future harm.

Slowly, painstakingly, she began to rebuild. She rediscovered her love for music, a passion that had been buried beneath layers of fear and self-doubt. She started writing again, pouring her emotions, her experiences, her anger, and her pain into her songs. The music became her therapy, her voice, her means of catharsis. The melodies flowed freely, the lyrics raw and honest, reflecting her journey, her struggles, and her unwavering resolve.

She found solace in the simplicity of creating, losing herself in the rhythm and harmony, finding a sense of purpose and meaning in the act of self-expression. Her songs were no longer just about love and heartbreak; they were anthems of resilience, testimonials of survival, stories of overcoming adversity. They were a testament to her strength, her unwavering spirit, her refusal to be silenced.

She began performing again, cautiously at first, in small, intimate venues, sharing her music with a select audience. The response was overwhelming, the warmth and support she received providing a much-needed boost to her confidence. Her music resonated with those who had endured similar struggles, providing a sense of community, a shared experience, a voice for the voiceless.

Her journey wasn't about revenge or retribution. It was about healing, about self-discovery, about finding her own voice and using it to empower others. She transformed her pain into purpose, turning her experience into a force for positive change. She dedicated her music to raising awareness about the issues she had encountered, speaking out against exploitation, advocating for better protection for artists, and demanding greater accountability within the industry.

She collaborated with organizations dedicated to empowering women in the music industry, mentoring young artists, sharing her experiences, and offering guidance to those navigating similar challenges. She became a beacon of hope, a symbol of resilience, a champion for social justice.

She used her platform to advocate for criminal justice reform, sharing her story, highlighting the systemic issues that had contributed to her vulnerability, and pushing for policies that would protect others from experiencing similar trauma. Her advocacy reached beyond the confines of the music industry, extending to broader societal issues, amplifying the voices of those who had been marginalized and silenced.

Her story became a powerful narrative, one that resonated far beyond the confines of the legal battles. It was a story of resilience, of empowerment, of transforming pain into purpose. It was a story that inspired hope, that sparked change, that amplified voices, and that offered a path to healing for countless others.

Her relationship with Big D remained strained, a complex tapestry of animosity and grudging respect. They never reconciled, never truly forgave each other, but they shared a common understanding of the consequences of their actions. They were bound by a shared history, a shared trauma, but their paths diverged, heading towards vastly different futures. There was no forgiveness, no reconciliation, only a silent acknowledgment of their shared past and a tacit understanding that each had found a path to their own redemption.

Serena's journey was a testament to the human spirit's ability to overcome adversity, to transform pain into purpose, and to find strength in the face of overwhelming challenges. Her story was not just about her personal healing; it was a call to action, a demand for justice, a beacon of hope for those who felt silenced, marginalized, and powerless. She found her voice, not through revenge, but through self-discovery, resilience, and the unwavering commitment to making a positive impact on the world. Her music, her activism, her advocacy, all became interwoven threads in the rich tapestry of her redemption, a testament to the enduring power of the human spirit. Her story was a powerful reminder that even in the darkest of times, the human spirit can find its way to the light.

The scars remained, etched deep into her soul, reminders of the battles fought and won. But they were also badges of honor, symbols of her resilience, testament to her journey from victim to victor. She carried them with dignity, with purpose, knowing that her story would inspire others, offering solace, hope, and a testament to the enduring power of the human spirit. Her journey, far from being over, had just begun. The road ahead remained long and uncertain, but Serena walked it with a newfound strength, a clarified purpose, and a voice that would echo through the years to come. Her music, once a tool for expressing pain, had now become a weapon for change, a symbol of hope, a force for good in a world that desperately needed it. And in her transformation, she became a beacon of inspiration for others navigating their own complex journeys towards healing and self-discovery. The whispers of her past, once threatening to consume her, were now transformed into a symphony of resilience, echoing her strength and her undeniable impact on the world.

The dust settled, leaving behind a landscape scarred by ambition and betrayal. Big D's empire, once a symbol of his relentless climb from the Chicago streets, lay in ruins. The federal investigation, sparked by Serena's accusations, had exposed a rot that went deeper than anyone had imagined. The trial, a spectacle of legal maneuvering and emotional outbursts, had become a microcosm of the industry itself: a brutal battleground where loyalty was a fleeting commodity and success came at a steep price.

Big D's fall wasn't simply a consequence of Serena's courage; it was the culmination of years of unchecked power, ruthless ambition, and a profound disregard for the human cost of his success. He'd built his empire on a foundation of questionable ethics, fueled by a hunger that consumed everything in its path. The legal battles had been expensive, draining his resources, and the public's perception of him had shifted from powerful mogul to disgraced executive. The once loyal employees and artists who flocked to his label had scattered, leaving him isolated, a king deposed. The weight of his actions pressed down on him, heavier than any legal sentence.

The legacy of his actions extended far beyond the courtroom. The artists he'd exploited, the lives he'd damaged, the trust he'd betrayed – these formed a silent chorus that echoed long after the gavel fell. The investigation had unearthed a trail of broken promises, exploited talent, and systematic manipulation. The details, laid bare for all to see, painted a disturbing portrait of an industry built on precarious relationships and a culture of silence. The silence, once a shield, now became a damning indictment of the systemic issues plaguing the music industry.

For Serena, the victory felt hollow. While she had achieved justice, the process had exacted a heavy toll. The psychological wounds ran deep, the scars invisible yet ever-present. The initial sense of triumph morphed into a haunting loneliness, a stark realization of the price she'd paid. The outpouring of public support had waned, leaving her to confront the emotional aftermath alone. She learned a painful lesson: that justice isn't always synonymous with healing.

The lessons learned were profound and far-reaching. For Big D, it was a stark reckoning with the consequences of his choices. The relentless pursuit of wealth and power had blinded him to the moral compass he'd abandoned long ago. His fall wasn't merely a business failure; it was a spiritual bankruptcy, a testament to the corrosive nature of unchecked ambition. The glittering facade of his success had crumbled, revealing the emptiness at its core. His story serves as a cautionary tale, a reminder that the pursuit of wealth, achieved at the expense of others, is ultimately a hollow victory.

Serena's journey was one of resilience and self-discovery. While she had confronted and overcome the trauma of exploitation, her fight was far from over. She transformed her experience into a catalyst for change, becoming a voice for others who had been silenced and marginalized. Her activism, born from personal pain, became a powerful force for positive transformation within the music industry. Her music, previously a tool for self-expression, became a powerful weapon against injustice.

The narrative transcends the confines of a single story, revealing systemic issues within the music industry. The exploration of the industry's dark underbelly, its exploitation of vulnerable artists, its culture of silence, and its power dynamics, brought to light the urgent need for reform. The story serves not only as a testament to the human spirit's capacity for resilience but also as a call to action. It highlights the need for greater accountability, for transparent contracts, for robust legal protections, and for a culture shift that prioritizes the well-being of artists over profit.

The aftermath extended beyond the legal battles. The ripple effects of Big D's actions and Serena's revelations continued to shake the foundations of the industry. Other artists, emboldened by Serena's courage, began to speak out about their own experiences of exploitation and abuse. Investigations into other record labels followed, revealing a widespread pattern of predatory practices. The culture of silence that had protected the abusers for so long began to crumble, replaced by a growing movement for change.

The story also explores the complexities of justice and redemption. While Serena found a measure of justice in the courtroom, the true redemption came from her healing journey and her subsequent advocacy work. She found strength not through retribution, but through empowerment, using her voice to amplify the experiences of others and fight for systemic change. Big D's situation served as a contrast, highlighting the difficulty of finding redemption after such profound betrayal and exploitation. His path towards rehabilitation, if possible at all, would be far more arduous, requiring genuine remorse and a complete overhaul of his values. The story leaves the reader contemplating the meaning of justice, its limitations, and the long and difficult road towards genuine redemption.

The legacy of this ordeal was not solely defined by legal outcomes or financial repercussions. It impacted the lives of countless individuals, shaping their perceptions of the music industry and its inherent power dynamics. The emotional scars left behind – the trauma, the betrayal, the disillusionment –

served as powerful reminders of the human cost of unchecked ambition and exploitation.

Ultimately, the narrative is a complex exploration of human nature, highlighting both the capacity for immense cruelty and extraordinary resilience. It is a story that underscores the importance of accountability, justice, and the transformative power of speaking truth to power. It is a story that resonates beyond the world of music, offering a cautionary tale about the seductive nature of power and the enduring importance of empathy, integrity, and moral responsibility in all aspects of life. The lessons learned extend far beyond the courtroom, challenging us to confront the shadows within ourselves and the systems that perpetuate injustice. The story's resonance stems from its unflinching portrayal of the human condition, its exploration of ambition's pitfalls, and its testament to the power of resilience, ultimately leaving the reader to contemplate the complexities of justice, forgiveness, and the enduring quest for redemption. The silence that once shrouded the industry is broken, replaced by a chorus of voices demanding change, and in that change lies the possibility of a brighter, more just future. The echoes of the past will remain, but the future holds the promise of a more equitable and ethical music industry, built on the foundations of justice, transparency, and respect for the human spirit.

## Chapter 5: New Beginnings

The air in the small, sparsely furnished office felt different. Gone was the opulent mahogany and the intimidating artwork of his former empire. This space, a converted warehouse unit in a less glamorous part of Chicago, hummed with a different energy – one of quiet determination, not aggressive ambition. Big D, stripped of his tailored suits and replaced with a simple button-down shirt and jeans, sat at a repurposed desk, a stark contrast to the mahogany behemoth that once symbolized his power. He stared out the window, the city sprawling before him, a landscape he once dominated, now a canvas upon which he had to paint a new future.

The trial had left him hollowed out, a shell of the man he once was. The weight of his actions, the betrayal of those who trusted him, pressed down on him, a constant, aching reminder of his past mistakes. The legal battles had drained not just his financial resources but his very soul. The loss wasn't merely financial; it was a profound loss of self-respect, a shattering of the carefully constructed persona he had cultivated for years. He had lost more than money and power; he had lost his integrity.

His initial attempts at rebuilding were hesitant, almost tentative. The connections he had cultivated over years, built on mutual self-interest and shady deals, had evaporated. The artists he once courted now shunned him, their distrust justified by his past actions. He found himself alienated, an outcast in the very industry he had once ruled. The whispers followed him, a constant reminder of his downfall.

The sting of failure was bitter, the humiliation profound. But beneath the surface, something had shifted. The crucible of his downfall had forged a change within him. The remorse wasn't a convenient strategy for regaining public favor; it was a genuine reckoning with the choices he'd made.

He began small, focusing on mentoring young, aspiring musicians from his old neighborhood. He offered them guidance, not exploitation. He shared his knowledge of the music business, not his manipulative tactics. He spoke of the importance of authenticity, of respecting the creative process, of valuing human relationships over profit. These were lessons he hadn't learned until he had lost everything. He started offering workshops, teaching aspiring songwriters the craft, guiding them through the challenges of the industry. His approach was radically different: collaboration, not coercion; mentorship, not manipulation; ethical practices, not exploitative ones.

His new venture wasn't about building a record label empire. It was about fostering a community of artists, supporting their growth, and ensuring they were treated fairly. He established a non-profit organization, providing resources and legal assistance to young musicians from disadvantaged backgrounds, offering them the kind of support and guidance he himself had lacked. He established fair contracts, transparency in deals, and a commitment to protecting the rights of the artists he worked with. His focus shifted from maximizing profits to maximizing potential. It was a slow, arduous process, a stark contrast to the rapid ascent he experienced in his previous life. He worked tirelessly, pouring his energy into this new mission, rebuilding his life brick by brick, choice by choice.

He wasn't seeking redemption in the eyes of the public; he sought it within himself. He understood that regaining public trust would take time, perhaps years, but he was committed to the path he had chosen. This new approach wasn't a mere public relations strategy; it was a reflection of his changed values, a testament to his commitment to a different path.

His new business ventures proved challenging but ultimately rewarding. He found success not in grand schemes and lucrative deals, but in the small victories – the success of his mentees, the growth of his non-profit, the gradual rebuilding of his reputation. The money was less, the power considerably diminished, but the satisfaction was immeasurable. He was no longer a king, but he was finally a man of integrity.

He invested in local artists, nurturing their talent and guiding them towards sustainable careers. He established partnerships with community organizations, providing workshops, mentorship programs, and recording studio access to underserved communities. He focused on building relationships based on mutual respect and trust, a sharp contrast to the transactional relationships that had characterized his former business dealings. He understood that true success wasn't measured by financial wealth but by the positive impact he had on the lives of others.

The challenges were constant. He faced skepticism, distrust, and the lingering shadow of his past. Some remained unconvinced of his genuine change, seeing his new ventures as a thinly veiled attempt at reclaiming his former status. But he persisted, driven by a sense of purpose that had been absent during his years of unchecked ambition. He understood that true redemption wasn't about erasing the past but about making amends for his mistakes and creating a positive future.

He found solace in the small successes – a mentee's first successful gig, a grant secured for his non-profit, a letter from a former artist expressing gratitude for his changed approach. These were the rewards that fueled his commitment, the milestones that validated his new path. His story became a testament to the transformative power of remorse and the enduring human capacity for change. He had lost everything, but in losing everything, he had found something far more valuable: a sense of purpose, a renewed sense of self, and a commitment to living a life guided by ethical principles.

His journey was far from over. The road to redemption is long and arduous, but Big D was committed to walking it. He knew that he couldn't erase his past mistakes, but he could work tirelessly to create a future where his actions reflected his changed values. His story, once a cautionary tale of unchecked ambition, was slowly evolving into a narrative of resilience, redemption, and the possibility of finding a new purpose in the wake of profound failure. The music industry, once a symbol of his past transgressions, now served as a stage for his transformation. The once-silent chorus of his past mistakes was slowly being replaced by a new melody—one of hope, regeneration, and a commitment to a future built on integrity and empathy. The empire he'd lost was gone, but he was building something new, something real, something built on the foundations of genuine remorse and ethical conduct. The city that once saw him as a fallen king now watched him, slowly but surely, reclaim his humanity, not through power, but through purpose.

The first person Big D sought out was Serena. Finding her wasn't easy. She'd vanished after the trial, disappearing into the anonymity of the city, a ghost in the very industry she'd once graced. He'd tracked her down through a mutual friend, a former colleague who, surprisingly, still held a flicker of loyalty. The meeting was arranged in a quiet corner cafe, far removed from the glitz and glamour of the city's hotspots. Serena arrived late, her eyes shadowed, her once vibrant energy dimmed. She looked fragile, almost broken. The vibrant star he remembered was replaced by a woman carrying the weight of the world on her shoulders.

He didn't offer excuses, didn't attempt to justify his actions. He simply sat across from her, his gaze unwavering, and listened. He listened to the pain in her voice, the anger that still simmered beneath the surface. He heard the recounting of her struggles, the betrayal she'd felt, the dreams he'd shattered. He listened without interruption, allowing her to express her hurt, her rage, her disillusionment. It was a painful process, a gut-wrenching confrontation with the consequences of his actions, a stark reminder of the damage he'd inflicted.

He didn't expect forgiveness. He didn't even plead for it. He merely offered a sincere apology, a heartfelt expression of remorse, devoid of self-serving justifications. He spoke of the emptiness he'd felt during his downfall, the profound loneliness that had accompanied his loss of power and wealth. He acknowledged the depth of his betrayal, the irreparable damage he'd done to her career and her trust. He spoke of his journey of self-reflection, the hard lessons he'd learned, the changes he'd made. He spoke not of the empire he'd lost, but of the man he'd become.

The conversation stretched over hours, fueled by strong coffee and a palpable tension. There were moments of intense emotion, moments of silence punctuated by the clinking of cups. Tears flowed freely, not just from Serena, but from Big D as well. He faced the full weight of his actions, accepting responsibility without reservation. He didn't expect a sudden reconciliation, a magical erasure of the past. He understood that healing would take time, that trust would need to be earned, not demanded. He left the cafe with a feeling of profound exhaustion, but also a sense of liberation. He'd faced his demons, and in doing so, he'd begun the process of making amends.

His next step was to approach his former associates, the men who had been complicit in his actions. These were the harder conversations, laden with resentment and suspicion. He had to navigate a minefield of mistrust, facing accusations of insincerity and manipulation. Many saw his attempts at reconciliation as a calculated maneuver, a desperate attempt to salvage his reputation. He didn't flinch. He presented a clear picture of his altered perspective, emphasizing his commitment to ethical conduct and fair practices. He acknowledged their role in his downfall, taking responsibility for his part in creating a culture of exploitation. He wasn't seeking absolution; he was seeking understanding, a chance to demonstrate the genuineness of his transformation.

Some were receptive. Others remained deeply skeptical, unwilling to forgive his past actions. But the act of reaching out, the sincere attempt to mend broken relationships, was its own reward. He discovered a surprising resilience in the face of rejection, a strength that stemmed from his newfound sense of purpose. The process of reconciliation was challenging, arduous, and deeply personal. It was a journey of self-discovery, a confrontation with his own flaws, and a testament to the enduring power of human connection. He understood that rebuilding trust wouldn't be easy. It demanded humility, consistency and time.

He discovered the need to address the systemic issues that had fueled his past behavior. He realized he hadn't simply acted alone; the corrupt structure of the industry had allowed—even encouraged—his exploitative practices. He started advocating for fairer contracts, more transparent dealings, and increased protections for artists. He invested time and resources into lobbying for legislation that would promote ethical conduct within the music industry. This wasn't merely an act of amends, it was a commitment to creating a more just and equitable system. This advocacy work became another crucial component of his path toward healing.

His efforts to rebuild relationships also extended to his family. His mother, a woman who had endured years of his neglect and disappointment, needed time. He spent countless hours rebuilding the bonds that had been severed by his ambition. He shared his new life, his commitment to making amends, his efforts toward creating a different future. He faced their skepticism and distrust, their anger and disappointment, and in doing so, he faced himself. It wasn't a simple process of reconciliation; it was a profound re-evaluation of his relationship with his family, and a testament to the enduring power of familial love. The road to mending those fractured bonds was still long but now it was paved with honesty and self-awareness.

Big D's journey of forgiveness and reconciliation wasn't just a personal endeavor; it became a public narrative, a story of transformation. His changed approach resonated with many within the industry, inspiring other record label executives and artists to consider more ethical ways of conducting business. He became a symbol of second chances, a testament to the human capacity for change, a man who lost everything but found himself in the process of rebuilding.

His story became a case study, a complex example of the complexities of redemption. It wasn't a fairytale ending, a simple resolution of conflict. It was an ongoing process, a daily commitment to ethical conduct, a constant work in progress. His story is a reminder that forgiveness and reconciliation are not one-time events but a sustained practice. His redemption wouldn't erase his past, but it would undoubtedly shape his future. The once-powerful mogul, now a quiet force for positive change, demonstrated the strength of his character, not in the wealth he'd amassed, but in the lives he was changing, the relationships he was mending, and the legacy he was now creating. The city watched him, not just as a fallen king, but as a man striving for redemption, proving that even the most damaged souls can find a path to healing and a future built on integrity. His transformation served as a powerful reminder that true success isn't measured in riches, but in the depth of one's character and the integrity of one's actions.

The air in the recording studio hummed with a controlled energy, a stark contrast to the chaotic whirlwind of her previous life. Serena, bathed in the soft glow of studio lights, moved with a newfound grace, her voice a powerful instrument weaving its magic through the microphones. Gone was the shadow of fear, the lingering resentment, the pervasive sense of vulnerability that had clung to her like a shroud. In its place bloomed a radiant confidence, a self-assuredness that radiated from her every pore. This wasn't the Serena who had been silenced, controlled, manipulated. This was Serena reborn, a phoenix rising from the ashes of betrayal.

She hummed a melody, a low, soulful tune that resonated deep within her. The producer, a young, sharp-eyed man named Marcus, nodded approvingly, his fingers tapping a steady rhythm on the control panel. He'd been handpicked by Serena, a collaborative spirit who understood her vision, her need for autonomy, her desire to express her artistry without compromise. Marcus wasn't just a producer; he was a partner, a collaborator, a fellow artist who understood the nuances of her craft, the emotional depth she poured into her music. He listened, he guided, he encouraged, always ensuring her creative freedom remained paramount.

Her new album, tentatively titled "Phoenix," was a testament to her resilience, a powerful narrative of struggle, survival, and ultimately, triumph. The lyrics, raw and honest, poured out of her, each word a shard of her experience, each note a testament to her strength. She sang of betrayal, of broken trust, of the pain of silencing, and of the agonizing fight for her own voice. But interwoven within the pain was a message of empowerment, a celebration of self-discovery, a resounding anthem of independence. It wasn't just a collection of songs; it was a journey, a cathartic release, a testament to her indomitable spirit.

The songs themselves were a stunning evolution of her style. While retaining the soulful essence that had captivated her audience, she explored new sonic landscapes, experimenting with rhythms and instrumentation, pushing the boundaries of her artistic expression. She incorporated elements of hip-hop, R&B, and even touches of electronic music, creating a rich and diverse soundscape that reflected her multifaceted personality. This wasn't a simple replication of her past success; it was a bold, innovative leap forward, a testament to her growth as an artist.

The recording process was a collaborative effort, a harmonious blend of creative energies. Marcus encouraged experimentation, challenging her to push her boundaries, to explore uncharted territories. He celebrated her strengths, offering gentle guidance when necessary, but always respecting her artistic vision. The studio sessions were filled with laughter, intense creative discussions, and moments of profound emotional connection. They were far removed from the tense, controlling atmosphere of her previous work environment. This was a sanctuary of creativity, a space where Serena could be herself, without fear of judgment or manipulation.

Beyond the recording studio, Serena's triumph extended into every aspect of her professional life. She had secured a new management team, a group of sharp, ethical individuals who understood the importance of protecting artists' rights and promoting creative freedom. They were her allies, her advocates, her partners in navigating the complex world of the music industry. She carefully reviewed every contract, ensuring fair compensation and artistic control, a stark contrast to the exploitative deals she had endured in the past. She had learned her lessons well.

Her newfound independence also extended to her public image. She consciously crafted a persona that reflected her values, her strength, her resilience. She embraced authenticity, rejecting the manufactured image that had once been imposed upon her. She spoke openly about her experiences, her struggles, her triumphs, inspiring other artists to demand better treatment, to fight for their rights, to embrace their true selves. She became a vocal advocate for fair contracts, transparent dealings, and increased protections for artists within the industry. Her public pronouncements resonated with millions, her story becoming a beacon of hope, an example of how one person could overcome adversity and emerge triumphant.

Her influence wasn't limited to her own career; she actively mentored up-and-coming artists, sharing her experiences and guiding them through the treacherous landscape of the music industry. She became a role model, a mentor, a leader, inspiring a new generation of musicians to prioritize their artistic integrity and their personal well-being. She established a foundation to support young artists from disadvantaged backgrounds, providing resources and opportunities that she herself had lacked. This wasn't just about personal success; it was about building a more just and equitable system within the music industry.

The release of "Phoenix" was a watershed moment. The album debuted at number one on the charts, smashing records and garnering critical acclaim. Serena's voice, now stronger and more resonant than ever, filled the airwaves, resonating with millions of listeners who were captivated by her story, her music, and her unwavering spirit. The album wasn't just a commercial success; it was a cultural phenomenon, a testament to her artistic genius and her indomitable spirit. It was a celebration of survival, a testament to the power of resilience, and a resounding affirmation of her triumph over adversity.

The accolades poured in: Grammy nominations, awards from industry organizations, and endless praise from critics. But Serena remained grounded, focused on her art, her message, and her commitment to positive change. She understood that her success wasn't merely about personal achievement; it was about inspiring others, about creating a better future for aspiring artists, about using her platform to advocate for justice and equality.

Her public appearances were no longer fraught with anxiety and fear; instead, she commanded the stage with confidence, her presence radiating strength and grace. She connected with her audience on a deeply personal level, sharing her story, offering inspiration, and reminding everyone that even in the darkest of times, hope can prevail. She became a symbol of resilience, a testament to the human spirit's capacity to overcome adversity and emerge stronger than ever before. Her concerts were filled with energy, passion, and a profound sense of connection between the artist and her devoted fans.

The transformation wasn't just external; it was deeply internal. The scars of her past remained, but they had become a part of her narrative, a source of strength and wisdom. She had learned to embrace her vulnerabilities, to transform pain into art, and to use her experiences to inspire and empower others. She had found peace, not by forgetting the past, but by understanding it, by accepting it, and by using it to fuel her journey toward healing and self-discovery.

Serena's journey wasn't a fairy tale; it was a gritty, honest portrayal of resilience and triumph in the face of adversity. It was a story that resonated deeply with her audience, reminding them that even in the darkest of times, hope remains, and that the human spirit is capable of incredible feats of strength and perseverance. Her success wasn't just a measure of commercial achievement, but a testament to her character, her courage, and her unwavering commitment to her art and to creating a better world for others. Her triumph was a resounding victory, not just for herself, but for all those who had ever felt silenced, unheard, or underestimated. It was a triumph that resonated far beyond the music industry, a powerful reminder of the enduring power of the human spirit and the transformative potential of art. The city, once again, watched her, but this time, with admiration, respect, and perhaps a touch of awe. This was not just the end of a chapter; this was the start of a new era.

The federal investigation, the betrayal by Serena, the near-collapse of his empire – these events hadn't simply shaken Big D; they had shattered him. The man who clawed his way from the South Side streets to the penthouse suite, the man who built his success on ruthless ambition and an unwavering will to win, was gone. In his place stood a man humbled, stripped bare, forced to confront the consequences of his actions, the wreckage of his unchecked ego. The opulent trappings of his success – the sprawling mansion, the fleet of luxury cars, the constant entourage – felt suddenly hollow, insignificant in the face of the potential loss of everything he held dear.

His initial response had been one of furious denial, a desperate attempt to cling to the illusion of control. He'd thrown himself into work, doubling down on his efforts to salvage his reputation, to prove to the world, and perhaps more importantly to himself, that he was still in command. He'd spent sleepless nights poring over legal documents, strategizing with his lawyers, trying to outmaneuver the federal investigators. But the exhaustion was crippling, the relentless pressure a vise around his chest. The façade of invincibility, carefully constructed over years of relentless struggle, began to crumble.

The cracks appeared first in subtle ways: a missed meeting, a snapped word to a longtime associate, a rare moment of vulnerability shown to his mother. Then came the breakthrough – a moment of clarity, a shattering realization of the destructive path he'd been following. It wasn't a sudden epiphany, but a gradual dawning of understanding, a slow, painful process of self-reflection. He began to see the cost of his ambition, the damage he had inflicted on others in his relentless pursuit of success. Serena's accusations, though painful and damaging, had served as a crucial catalyst, forcing him to confront the truth about himself, the flaws that had driven him to the brink.

He started small. He spent time with his mother, something he'd neglected for years, consumed by the demands of his business. He listened to her stories, stories he'd previously dismissed as insignificant in his pursuit of wealth and power. He saw the sacrifices she had made for him, the years of struggle and hardship she'd endured to give him a chance at a better life. Her love, unwavering and unconditional, became a lifeline, reminding him of the values he had lost sight of amidst his ascent. It was in her quiet wisdom that he started to piece together the man he wanted to become.

His commitment to social responsibility emerged from this newfound humility. He established a foundation to provide educational opportunities for underprivileged youth in Chicago, the city that had shaped him. He used his influence to advocate for criminal justice reform, a cause close to his heart given his own experiences with the legal system. He poured resources into mentoring programs for young entrepreneurs, sharing his knowledge and expertise, hoping to guide others toward success without the pitfalls he had encountered. It wasn't about philanthropy for show; it was a sincere commitment to repairing the damage he had caused and giving back to the community that had given him so much.

The transformation was evident in his business practices as well. He implemented stricter ethical guidelines, ensuring fair treatment of artists and employees. He invested in developing young talent, providing them with the support and resources they needed to flourish. Gone were the days of cutthroat competition and exploitative contracts. He fostered a culture of collaboration and mutual respect, recognizing the value of teamwork and the importance of supporting his associates. His empire, once built on ruthless ambition, now stood on a foundation of integrity and fairness.

His relationship with Serena was a testament to his transformation. He'd made amends, apologizing sincerely for his past behavior and acknowledging the harm he had caused. It wasn't a simple reconciliation; it was a difficult process of rebuilding trust, of demonstrating genuine remorse and a commitment to change. He listened to her, truly listened, understanding the depth of her pain and the reasons behind her accusations. He acknowledged his role in silencing her voice, in exploiting her talent for his own gain. He learned to value her artistry, her resilience, and her strength. He supported her, not as a commodity but as a fellow human being, someone deserving of respect and recognition.

The legal battles were still ongoing, the shadow of the investigation still loomed, but Big D faced them with a different mindset. He cooperated fully with the authorities, providing information and accepting responsibility for his actions. He wasn't seeking to evade justice; he was seeking redemption. He understood that his past couldn't be erased, but it could be atoned for. His legal team, initially surprised by his change of heart, became his allies in his quest for redemption. The legal process, once a source of fear and anxiety, became a path toward healing and accountability.

His public image, once carefully crafted to project an image of untouchable power, underwent a complete overhaul. He spoke publicly about his transformation, sharing his story with a candor that surprised many. He didn't try to minimize his mistakes or deflect blame; he owned his actions, admitting his flaws and highlighting the lessons he had learned. His honesty resonated with the public, many of whom admired his willingness to confront his past and commit to positive change. The city that once celebrated his rise now witnessed his fall and subsequent transformation with a curious mixture of awe and admiration.

This wasn't merely a change of image; it was a fundamental shift in his identity. The man who had climbed the ladder of success by any means necessary was replaced by someone dedicated to building a legacy of integrity and social responsibility. He had finally understood that true success wasn't measured in wealth or power, but in the positive impact he had on the lives of others. The journey hadn't been easy, the scars remained, but his transformation was complete. He had emerged from the ashes, not as a phoenix, but as a changed man, a better man. The city that once watched his rise with a mixture of envy and awe, now watched his transformation with a newfound respect, a silent acknowledgment of the profound journey he had undertaken. Big D's story wasn't just about the rise and fall of a mogul, it was about the power of redemption, the potential for change, and the enduring strength of the human spirit. His story became a lesson, a testament to the fact that even the most flawed among us can find redemption, can choose a different path, and can, in the end, become better versions of ourselves. The new beginnings weren't just for Serena; they were for Big D, too. He had finally found peace, not in the fleeting pleasures of success, but in the enduring satisfaction of a life lived with integrity and purpose. The empire he'd rebuilt was not just a business; it was a reflection of his transformed soul, a testament to the possibility of a second chance. The city, once a stage for his ambition, now served as a witness to his profound and lasting transformation.

The courtroom air, thick with the scent of old wood and hushed anticipation, held a different weight now. The tension that had previously crackled with animosity had dissipated, replaced by a quiet understanding. Big D sat, his posture straighter than it had been in months, his gaze steady. The trial, a protracted ordeal that had threatened to consume him, was nearing its end. The plea bargain, a bitter pill to swallow, had been accepted. He'd admitted to tax evasion and some lesser charges, sparing Serena further anguish and preventing the complete collapse of his empire. The price was steep – a hefty fine, community service, and a period of probation – but it was a price he was willing to pay. This wasn't about escaping consequences; it was about accepting responsibility and moving forward.

The judge's gavel fell, punctuating the end of a chapter in his life. As he left the courthouse, the weight of the past seemed to lift, replaced by a lighter burden, the weight of expectation and responsibility. The flash of cameras, the murmur of reporters, barely registered. His focus was inward, on the future, on the path he'd chosen. The city, once a backdrop for his ambition, now felt different, almost…familiar. The familiar rumble of the El train, the scent of deep-dish pizza, the rhythm of street life, these were the constants that had remained, grounding him in a reality beyond the opulent world he'd built and almost lost.

His commitment to the community blossomed. The Big D Foundation, initially conceived as a damage-control measure, grew into a powerful force for positive change. He poured his energy and resources into creating opportunities for young people, providing scholarships, mentoring programs, and job training initiatives. He partnered with local schools, establishing after-school programs focused on music production, entrepreneurship, and conflict resolution. He wasn't just writing checks; he was actively involved, sharing his experiences and knowledge, guiding the next generation with the wisdom born of his own hard-won lessons. He wasn't just a philanthropist; he was a mentor, a guide, a symbol of redemption. His actions spoke louder than any press release ever could.

His relationship with Serena evolved beyond the courtroom drama. Their professional partnership, once marred by exploitation and mistrust, transformed into a collaborative creative force. She had released a powerful album, her music echoing with resilience and strength, reflecting her journey through the trials and tribulations. Big D, now a supportive force in her career, guided her with patience and respect, providing her with the resources and freedom to express herself authentically. He understood the value of her voice, and he was determined to amplify it. Their collaborative spirit led to the creation of a joint project, a documentary showcasing the lives of young, aspiring musicians navigating the treacherous path of the music industry. Their combined efforts offered a unique perspective, a combination of the hard-earned wisdom and the raw talent which inspired many.

The record label underwent a complete overhaul. The cutthroat practices, the exploitative contracts, the win-at-all-costs mentality – all were gone. Instead, Big D fostered a culture of collaboration, mutual respect, and fair treatment. He empowered his employees, investing in their development, providing them with opportunities to grow and learn. The label became a breeding ground for creativity, innovation, and social responsibility. His commitment to ethical practices attracted both talented artists and ethically conscious investors, strengthening the label's reputation and stability. The old empire, built on ambition, had been replaced by a new one, built on integrity.

His personal life, once defined by isolation and ambition, bloomed. He spent more time with his mother, reconnecting with the woman who had sacrificed so much for him. He found solace in the simple pleasures of family, rediscovering the importance of genuine human connection. The expansive mansion still stood, but it felt different now. It was no longer a symbol of his wealth and power, but a home, a place of warmth, love, and tranquility.

Five years passed. Big D stood on the rooftop of his newly renovated office building, overlooking the city skyline. The city lights twinkled below, reflecting in the panoramic windows, painting the office in a vibrant, warm glow. He wasn't the same man who'd stood here five years prior, consumed by ambition and shrouded in the shadows of his past mistakes. He'd lost weight, his face less etched with the stress lines of constant battles. His eyes held a calmer strength, a wisdom honed by experience. He watched the sun dip below the horizon, casting long shadows across the city. It was a beautiful sight, a view that held a depth it didn't before.

The past was still a part of him, a constant reminder of the lessons learned, the mistakes made, and the path he'd traveled to reach this point. But it no longer defined him. He had emerged from the ashes, not as a phoenix, but as a man transformed, a man at peace with himself and the world around him. The journey had been arduous, marked by setbacks, betrayal, and self-doubt. But it had also been a journey of profound self-discovery, a testament to the resilience of the human spirit.

He looked out at the city, at the vibrant tapestry of lives unfolding below, and felt a profound sense of gratitude. He'd never forget where he came from, the harsh realities of the streets that had shaped him, the challenges he'd overcome. But he also recognized the power of redemption, the potential for change, the possibility of a second chance. His story was far from over. In fact, it was just beginning.

The new beginnings weren't just a chapter; they were a testament to his enduring spirit, a symbol of hope, not just for himself but for those he had vowed to help. The city, once a battleground for his ambition, had become a canvas for his redemption. His legacy wouldn't be defined by the opulence of his empire but by the lives he touched, the opportunities he created, and the positive change he inspired. The future was uncertain, filled with challenges, but he faced it with a newfound confidence, a quiet strength that came from within. He wasn't just surviving; he was thriving. He was Big D, and he was finally free. The city, once a witness to his rise and fall, now stood as a silent testament to his remarkable journey of transformation, a journey that offered a profound and enduring message of hope and redemption. The epilogue wasn't just the end of a story; it was the beginning of a legacy.

# Author

A. Abney grew up in Connecticut and worked many years in law enforcement. He has also authored several books including a memoir. During his time in law enforcement he investigated and helped solve thousands of criminal cases. Now he shares those experiences with you. His Apple podcast, PTSD: True Crime Stories, showcases crime stories inspired by actual events.

This book is dedicated to my family and friends who stood beside me and pushed me to go on. The road to success is long and lonely but you can make it through.

www.ingramcontent.com/pod-product-compliance
Lightning Source LLC
Chambersburg PA
CBHW060946050426
42337CB00052B/1617